tennis, anyone?

SECOND EDITION

DICK GOULD
Tennis Coach, Stanford University

 national press books

850 Hansen Way, Palo Alto, California

Library of Congress Catalog Card Number: 76-142367
International Standard Book Number: 0-87484-179-8 (paper)
                                    0-87484-180-1 (cloth)
Manufactured in the United States of America

Illustrations by Dick Keeble (photographs)
             Tina Wikstrom (figures)
             Nancy Sears (courts)

contents

PreFace

Discover tennis! Tennis is the most universàlly played of all sports. Its rules are the same the world over. It can be played by anyone within a short period of time, indoors or out, and with relatively inexpensive equipment.

It can be only moderately strenuous, or it can be the most demanding of sports. Herein lies its greatest value, for it affords a most enjoyable and stimulating way to keep physically fit.

More leisure time allows entire families to be attracted to tennis. The rapidly increasing availability of private and public courts at clubs, schools, and in cities is astounding. Largely because of expanded accessibility, tennis is more popular than ever before.

If you want to play tennis, resolve to learn to play it correctly and to the best of your ability. Remember, however, that there is no shortcut to mastery of tennis. The learning process will be tedious and discouraging. The complex nature of the game and the intricate skills involved account for the fact that it takes many years of hard, concentrated effort to become a good tennis player.

No matter how good you may become, you will never be satisfied with your success. But if you have the perseverance to keep trying, you will eventually profit from learning an extremely valuable and enjoyable avocation. May this book help to start you on your way!

strokes:
the weapons of tennis

GENERAL STROKE PRINCIPLES

As a prelude to our detailed discussion of tennis strokes, it is important that you understand several general principles upon which successful stroke production greatly depends.

Concentration

The first essential principle in learning tennis is concentration. Begin to master this principle by thinking only of tennis from the moment you walk on the court to the moment you leave. During play, concentrate on watching the ball. Two-thirds of all points lost in tennis are lost because the player does not watch the ball closely enough. Try to watch the ball so closely that you can see the label.

Drill

Place a tennis ball on the floor, and stare at it for 30 seconds. Think only of the ball and let nothing interrupt your thoughts. As you become more proficient, add some outside distraction (radio, television, etc.).

Simplicity

The tennis stroke is a smooth, continuous motion which allows the racket head to build increasing momentum. This momentum culminates at the moment of impact when all your stored power is unleashed at the ball.

Limit the variables   The more things you do, the greater the chance you will do one of them incorrectly. Try to keep from making any unnecessary or exaggerated movements. Apply the geometric axiom that the shortest distance between two points is a straight line.

Develop naturalness in the basic motions   No matter how simplified a motion may be, it may not seem natural to you the first few times you try it. However, repetition will increase your familiarity with a movement and will gradually make it easier to perform. Ultimately the action will become a habit, so that no conscious effort will be needed to perform the act. If you become discouraged, think of the analogy that may be drawn with a baby just learning to walk. He looks very awkward at first, and he has many moments of despair. In the end, however, performing this originally complex task becomes second nature.

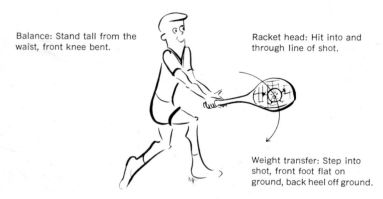

Balance: Stand tall from the waist, front knee bent.

Racket head: Hit into and through line of shot.

Weight transfer: Step into shot, front foot flat on ground, back heel off ground.

Balance

Stand up straight from the waist in order to finish shots freely, and especially to hit up with power. Relax, and flex the knees slightly. This will prepare you for the many low shots that necessitate a substantial bend in the knees.

Power

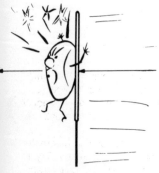

Power: Hit into and through line of shot.

Power in most sports is gained largely by transferring your weight in the direction you want the ball to go. Think of the pitcher in baseball, or the batter stepping into his pitch. In tennis, you should step into the line of the shot whenever possible, just before you bring the racket forward. The forward stepping foot receives all the weight, and is flat on the ground. The back heel is off the ground and bears almost no weight. The hitting face of the racket swings into and through the line of the shot (where the ball is intended to go). All your power is then unleashed in a straight line directed toward the level where you want the ball to clear the net.

Control

Control is the ability to regulate the speed and the direction of the ball. As a beginner your primary goal is consistency, and you should emphasize hitting softly. This allows you to develop a feel or "touch" of the ball on the racket and to "guide" the ball in the desired direction. It also allows gravity to exert a greater influence on the trajectory of the ball. It will help if you think of the person with whom you are playing as a partner, rather than an opponent.

As you gain more confidence in the production of the strokes, you will want to add more speed to your shots in an attempt to pressure your opponent into an error. Gravity now has proportionately less effect on the trajectory of the ball. However you can compensate by relying less on gravity and more on the spin of the ball to give you a controlled, yet forceful, shot.

If you have thrown or "pitched" a curve with a tennis ball, you are well aware of the manner in which spin affects the ball's flight. The type of spin desired (sidespin, underspin, or topspin) determines how the ball is stroked. The basic spin is topspin, in which the ball spins from top to bottom, making it curve downward into the court. Thus, in our initial discussion, we will be presenting the topspin drive stroke.

BEGINNING GROUND STROKES

Now we must apply the stroke guidelines of Concentration, Simplicity, Balance, Power, and Control to specific movements. We begin by dividing our swing into four basic categories, each with its own sub-categories:

Set Position	Forward Swing
Stance	Ready position
Forehand grip	Weight transfer
Backhand grip	and balance
Backswing	Point of contact
Forehand pivot	Follow-through
Backhand pivot	Recovery
Racket	
Moving to the ball	

As you practice the basic strokes, apply the general stroke principles you have just learned. The basic four categories above serve as checkpoints for the over-all motion. If these checkpoints are progressively correct, each successive part of the swing will be in order. Remember, however, that even though we speak of separate parts, the swing must be a smooth and continuous motion.

The principles of the forehand and backhand drive are nearly identical, except for the grip. For this reason, the discussion of the ground strokes will involve a simultaneous presentation of the basic forehand and backhand. Also the stroke instructions are written for a right-handed player, so if you are left-handed you will have to reverse the terminology.

Set Position

Stance   Position yourself one or two feet behind the center of the baseline, facing the direction from which the ball will be hit, and ready to move quickly in any direction. Place your feet about shoulder width apart. The weight is evenly distributed on the balls of your feet, and your knees are slightly bent.

Stance

Common Faults
1. *The knees are too stiff or too bent.*
2. *The body is bent over excessively from the waist.*

Forehand grip

Forehand grip   The throat of the racket is held lightly by your left hand so that the racket face is vertical to the ground as if it were "standing on edge." The racket is waist level, parallel to the ground, and pointing directly to the net.

Your right hand then grips the handle in a "shaking hands" position (the palm of the hand is neither turned up nor turned down). The "V" formed by the junction of the thumb and the index finger is squarely on the top of the racket handle. The thumb is completely around the racket handle; the fingers are slightly apart.

Backhand grip

Backhand grip   The left hand guides the racket back from the forehand position described above so that the racket is pointing to the left net post. Simultaneously, the right hand makes a quarter turn so that the palm of the hand is essentially on top of the racket handle. The bottom of the top knuckle of the index finger rests

Backhand grip

Footwork for pivot

Forehand pivot

Backhand pivot

Ball coming directly at
player.

Forehand

Backhand

squarely on top of the handle. The thumb gives additional support by assuming a diagonal position up the back of the handle. The fingers are slightly spread apart.

Common Faults

1. *The positioning of the "V" (forehand) or the top knuckle of the index finger (backhand) is incorrect.*
2. *The grip is a hammer grip—the fingers are too close together.*
3. *The grip is too limp.*
4. *The grip is not changed enough on the backhand.*

Backswing

The backswing is the part of the swing in which the racket travels from the set position to the ready position. The backswing is aided by a body pivot which turns your side to the net. This pivot permits you to move to the ball in a position facilitating the weight transfer into the shot.

Forehand pivot   The right foot steps in the direction you want to go as the shoulders turn: forward for a short ball, parallel to the baseline for most balls, and back only for a very deep ball.

Backhand pivot   The procedure is reversed: your left foot steps first in the direction you want the ball to go, which turns your right side toward the net and transfers your weight to the left foot. The turn is greater on the backhand, so that you are almost looking over your front shoulder at the ball.

Common Faults

1. *The initial step is often back from the ball.*
2. *The player's side fails to turn completely or turns too late.*

Racket   The racket is taken back simultaneously with the pivot. Try to have your backswing completed by the time the ball gets to your side of the net and, at the very latest, before it bounces. The backswing does not have to be unnaturally fast, provided it is begun early.

Circular backswing

Many players, especially beginners, find it easiest to take the racket straight back. There is no lost motion, for the racket moves back in a straight line. Keep the racket "standing on edge," parallel to the ground at waist level, by taking the tip of the racket head back first. In the *forehand*, the elbow stays comfortably close to the body and remains slightly bent as the arm follows the racket straight back to the ready position. For the *backhand*, the change of the grip puts the racket head in the correct position so that it is leading the arm back. The left hand is used to guide the racket head back to the ready position. The hitting arm is comfortably straight.

Common Faults

1. *The backswing is started too late. (The player runs several steps before starting his backswing.)*
2. *The wrist drags the racket back.*
3. *The elbow gets too far away from the body, preventing the racket from "standing on edge" and leading to excessive wrist movement.*
4. *The backswing is too high (too much waste motion).*
5. *The left hand lets go of the racket too soon on the backhand.*
6. *The arm is too straight on the forehand or too bent on the backhand.*

Most accomplished players use a *circular backswing* which tends to give the swing more continuity and rhythm. The tip of the racket head still goes back first, with the wrist and arm following. The racket head rises to eye level, the arm bends at the elbow (not wrist), and the body pivots to the side. The left hand helps on the backhand. Near the end of the backswing, the racket head starts to drop down as the arm straightens somewhat at the elbow (not by dropping the wrist) to the ready position.

The arc of this swing resembles the outline of a large egg. The racket simply traces the top of this egg.

Ready position

Ready position — shoulder-high ball

Ready position — low ball

Moving to the ball   On a straight backswing, the racket should go all the way back as you take your first pivot step. On a circular backswing, you should be completing the backswing as you are running toward the ball. You should arrive at the correct spot for hitting the ball soon enough to allow time to stop and set yourself, with the weight on your back foot.

Forward Swing

Ready position   You have now completed your backswing and have moved to the point where you expect to hit the ball—most often at the top of its bounce, and ideally at waist level. Your side is toward the net and your weight is either on your back foot or just starting to shift onto your front foot.

The racket is now pointing toward the back fence with the racket face still vertical to the ground ("standing on edge") the same way it will be on contact with the ball. For the forehand, the arm is comfortably bent. For the backhand, the arm is comfortably straight, with the left hand cradling the throat of the racket. Slight pressure exerted by the left thumb on the racket helps to keep the racket head low.

At the ready position for the forehand and backhand drive, the racket head must be slightly below the point at which you expect to contact the ball. (For a waist-high ball, the racket is parallel to the ground slightly below waist level. For a shoulder-high ball, the racket head is about shoulder level. For a knee-high ball, the racket head is below the knees.) If you must bend to hit a low ball, lower the shoulder that is away from the net. This will lower the racket head without causing you to drop your wrist. Bend over as little as possible from the waist, and avoid squatting down with the weight on both feet.

Common Faults

1. *The racket head is not far enough below the ball at the start of the forward swing.*
2. *The racket face "closes" over the ball, or turns "open" too much.*

You can determine the exact ready position by extending an imaginary line from (1) where you want to return the ball in relation to the top of the net, through point (2), where you expect to contact the ball. The extension of this imaginary line is point (3), the ready position for the racket head.

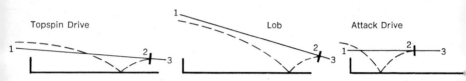

Topspin Drive   Lob   Attack Drive

Calculating the ready position:
1. Desired point of aim for the hit, in relation to the top of the net.
2. Anticipated point of contact with the ball.
3. Ready position — an extension of the line connecting points 1 and 2.

Most balls hit from the vicinity of the base line are *topspin drive* shots, with a safe net clearance. However, if the ball is a high and deep *lob*, you will probably be forced to retreat toward the back fence. In order to keep the ball deep to the opponent (or to hit over the head of an opponent who has moved to the net), you must return the ball higher than you would return a normal drive. The racket head starts much lower below the ball at the end of the backswing (ready position), and the racket face is "opened" so that it may remain perpendicular to the line of the shot.

If the ball lands short in the court, you should approach it quickly in order to hit the ball at the top of the bounce (*attack drive*), and to drive flat or straight through the line of the shot.

Weight transfer and balance   At the ready position, you have already run to the ball. You have stopped and your weight is on the back foot. You now transfer your weight into the line of shot, just as a batter would do as he

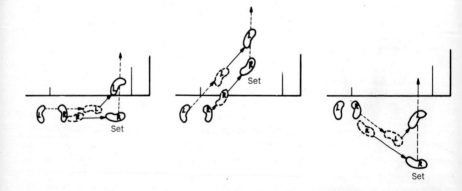

steps into the pitch. Your front foot is pointed approximately at a 45-degree angle with the baseline (toward the net post) as your weight shifts onto the front foot. The weight shift initiates the forward swing, and the two go together to produce an accurate and powerful shot.

As you step, the front knee bends slightly to absorb the weight. The bend is greater on a low ball, slighter on a high ball. In either case, the front knee is never stiff, and you stand straight from the waist. The front foot is flat on the ground; the heel of the back foot is off the ground, but the toe remains in contact with the court.

Point of contact   As the weight transfers onto the front foot, the racket begins to move directly forward from the ready position to the point of contact. The point of contact is in advance of the front foot. (The ball is contacted farther in front on the backhand than on the forehand.) As a general rule, the better the player, the farther in front the ball is contacted.

Point of contact for a high ball

The ball is easiest to hit when it is at waist level. If the ball drops lower than the waist, lower the strike zone by bending the knees. If the ball comes high and deep over the net, learn to anticipate a high bounce, and retreat far enough behind the baseline to enable the ball to drop down to waist level. (A more experienced player will often "take the ball on the rise" rather than retreat.)

Common Faults
1. *The player hits the ball too late (the ball gets too close to the body), usually because of a late backswing.*
2. *The wrist fails to remain firm on contact.*
3. *The elbow bends (and thus leads the racket to the ball) on the backhand.*
4. *The arm is too straight on the forehand.*

Point of contact for a waist-level ball

On contact, it is essential that the racket be held firmly in position, so that the racket head does not drop down. At the moment of impact on the forehand, the wrist is slightly "laid back" to keep the racket parallel to the net and help guide the ball straight instead of abruptly to the left. The farther in front the ball is contacted, the more the wrist will be naturally laid back.

Point of contact for a low ball

Follow-through The follow-through is the most important part of the entire stroke. It is also easiest to learn, since the racket comes to a complete stop at the end of the swing, allowing you to analyze the position to see if the checkpoints are in order.

As a beginner, force yourself to hold or "pose" momentarily on each follow-through. If you notice that your follow-through is not correct, change it so that it is right. Make correct stroking a habit. Draw an imaginary line from the point of contact to where you want the ball to go. The face of the racket continues out through the line as far as possible and up, until the racket comes to a gradual and complete stop. The racket comes up in follow-through to insure proper topspin to your drive shots.

Hint

Hit softly to your partner. It then takes longer for the ball to go to the other side of the net and return to you. This gives you time to check and correct your balance and racket position at the finish of your stroke. As a beginner you should hold your finish (and correct it) until the ball bounces on the other side of the net.

Develop touch and feel and softness by prolonging the swing itself as long as possible. Force yourself to keep the racket moving after you contact the ball, and come slowly to a stop.

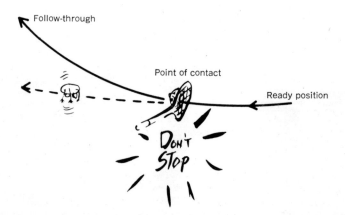

The position of the feet does not change during the forward swing. The front knee remains bent at the conclusion of the follow-through, and the weight is on the forward foot.

Important: Do not be timid. Force yourself to hit with a complete follow-through on each shot. It will pay off in the long run.

On the *forehand,* at the completion of follow-through check your position: you should be (1) standing straight from the waist, with the (2) front knee slightly bent and with the (3) front foot flat on the court and the (4) back heel off the court. The (5) arm is bent at the elbow in front of the chin, so that you are looking over your forearm to where you want the ball to go. The (6) wrist is at least at eye level, and is still firm, having neither slapped nor turned over. The wrist has very gradually straightened, so that now the racket and forearm are almost in line. The racket is pointing slightly above the top of the fence on the other side of the net. The (7) racket face is still "standing on edge."

When hitting the forehand, think of the racket as an extension of the arm. You are trying to catch the ball with the palm of your hand and lift it out over the net. This will help you to keep the wrist slightly laid back and to control the ball's direction. Most important, let the racket head do the work. The stroke must resemble a swing from the shoulder, not a push with the body or a slap with the wrist.

Common Faults

1. The racket fails to follow through far enough into the line of the shot.
2. The wrist fails to remain firm (it turns over or slaps at the ball).
3. The follow-through is not high enough (elbow in front of chin, wrist at least at eye level).
4. The body is too stiff—it fails to relax.
   a. The left shoulder dips over.
   b. The front knee straightens.
   c. The back foot swings forward, or slides backward on the finish.
   d. The back foot stays flat on the finish.

Forehand ground stroke

Backhand ground stroke

On the *backhand,* after contact, the (1) tip of the racket head should point gradually out into the direction of the hit and then continue out and up. Again, you should be (2) standing straight from the waist, with your side more toward the net than on the forehand and with the front knee slightly bent. The (3) front foot should be flat on the court, and the (4) back heel off the court.

The (5) wrist is at least at eye level, and the (6) racket is almost vertical to the ground instead of pointing to the opposite fence, since the grip is different than on the forehand. The wrist is still firm, having neither slapped nor turned over. The racket face is still "standing on edge," and the racket and arm are almost in line. (When hitting the backhand, think of the racket as an extension of the arm. You are trying to catch the ball on the racket and "lift" it out and over the net. The entire swing is from the shoulder.)

Common Faults

1. *The racket head drops (points to the opposite fence instead of straight into the air) because:*
   a. *The wrist doesn't remain firm.*
   b. *The body is too close to the ball.*
   c. *The knees don't bend enough for a low ball.*
   d. *The arm bends, and the elbow leads the swing.*
2. *The racket fails to follow through far enough into the line of the shot.*
3. *The follow-through is not high enough (the wrist should be at eye level and the racket vertical).*
4. *The body is too stiff.*
   a. *The head is anchored against the hitting shoulder.*
   b. *The front leg is straight (which causes a bending over from the waist).*
   c. *The back foot stays flat on the ground or slides back.*

Side shuffle step

Recovery

Return quickly to the set position, so you will be in position for the next shot. Use a side-shuffle step, such as a basketball player uses on defense.

**The Short Ball (Drive)
Illustrated**

Forehand

Backhand

The Deep Ball (Lob)
Illustrated

Forehand

Backhand

The toss

BEGINNING SERVE (FLAT)

The serve can be an extremely important weapon. You should work hard to develop one that is forceful and reliable.

Toss

A prerequisite of every good serve is a good toss. The tossing arm is comfortably extended so that the hand is at shoulder level, pointed in the direction of the serve, with the palm up. The ball is held in the fingers. The tossing arm drops toward the left thigh and then rises so that the arm is pointing straight up to the sky. Think of your tossing arm as an elevator: both drop straight down and go straight up.

Start with your weight on the back foot. The tossing arm should travel straight up (at a 90-degree angle with the court surface), pulling your weight onto the front foot. As late as possible in the tossing motion, "place" the ball into the air. Toss the ball above the forward foot, so that if you were to allow the ball to drop to the ground, it would land just in front of that foot. The ball should be tossed to a point just higher than the racket can reach. This means that the ball must only go about two feet above the extended tossing arm.

Common Faults

1. *The tossing hand lowers too much (to a point beside the leg instead of in front of it).*
2. *The ball is thrown too low.*
3. *The ball is thrown too far back (probably because it is "wristed" instead of "placed" into the air, or because the weight does not transfer forward).*
4. *The server rises onto the front toe, instead of keeping the foot flat (causing him to lean off balance).*

Backswing

You must coordinate the motion of the tossing arm with a relaxed, rhythmic motion of the racket arm, through the backswing and forward swing. To develop this rhythm and coordination, remember that both arms drop down together. As the racket passes the legs, both arms go up together. Practice this rhythm, saying: "down together;

Backswing, with arms rising.

Ready position, with arm
bending and racket
extending upward

up together." The racket arm should be completely re-laxed from the shoulder, so that the racket swings like the pendulum of a grandfather clock.

As the arms rise together, your weight transfers onto the front foot. When the racket and arm reach shoulder level, the palm of the racket hand is facing downward toward the court. As the arm reaches shoulder level, it starts to bend, so that in the ready position the elbow remains at shoulder level, and the forearm and racket point straight up into the air. It is important that your wrist not turn over or bend back on the backswing.

Forward Swing

The arm continues to bend as the racket drops behind the back, as if to scratch your back.

The elbow now leads forward, as if you were throwing a ball. The wrist follows the elbow forward, and the arm extends upward to the ball. This causes the body to rotate forward.

Use as little leg action as possible. Keep the front foot flat on the ground, and rotate the back foot on the toe.

Point of contact   The ball is hit with a pronounced wrist snap. The higher above you the ball is contacted, the better chance it has of clearing the net and going in. (If the racket had eyes, it could see more of the other court up high than from a lower position.)

Common Faults

1. *The weight fails to transfer onto the front foot.*
2. *The backswing and ball toss are uncoordinated (usually because the left hand drops too far to the side of the leg).*
3. *The backswing fails to be smooth and relaxed.*
4. *The wrist turns down during the backswing, thereby cramping the swing.*
5. *The server rises onto the left toe as the ball is thrown, thereby losing balance.*

Follow-through   The wrist snaps "over" the ball and hits out through the line of the shot. Then the racket head falls slowly down and over to the opposite side of your body.

Recovery

In the beginning you should try to keep your rear foot back, to check that your toss and balance are good. An advanced player often lets his rear foot cross over the line after contact with the ball. This helps him to regain balance if he has pushed up on his forward leg.

Common Faults

1. The hitting arm straightens too soon, causing a "pushing" motion.
2. The ball is allowed to drop too low, causing the swing and point of contact to be cramped.
3. Inadequate wrist action is used.
4. The follow-through is cramped, and not a full motion.

Service Pointers

Arc of the racket head from set position on through hit.

The serve must be a smooth, loose, continuous motion. Start the swing slowly and let the racket gain momentum. Two key words—"down" and "up"—describe the entire arc of the swing:

> Down—the racket drops down from the set position and points to the ground. The tossing hand drops preliminary to tossing the ball.

> Up—the racket head rises to above shoulder level. The tossing hand also rises to toss the ball.

> Down—the racket arm bends, causing the racket head to drop down behind the back, bringing the wrist almost into contact with the shoulder. The tossing arm drops out of the way, across the chest.

> Up—the racket head rises up high to contact the ball.

> Down—the racket head follows the ball out and then drops down to the opposite side of the body.

To help develop a rhythm in the serve, say to yourself as you swing: "down together; up together" (both arms); "behind the back" (racket drop); and "hit."

Don't attempt to hit the ball unless the throw is perfect. If you have trouble controlling the direction of the serve,

think of "catching" the ball in the strings of the racket. Think also of the face of the racket as the palm of your hand, and point the tip of the racket in the direction you want the ball to go.

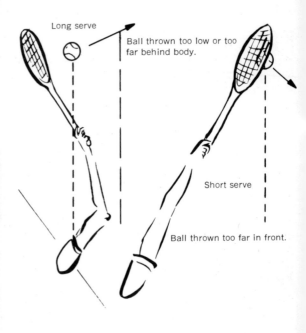

Long serve

Ball thrown too low or too far behind body.

Short serve

Ball thrown too far in front.

If your serves are going into the net, you may be throwing the ball too far forward or hitting down with your wrist rather than up. If the balls are going long, you may not be reaching up high enough to hit the ball, or perhaps you are throwing the ball too far behind your body.

The "Hammer-Nail" serve may help you if you are having difficulty coordinating the full swing. Eliminate the backswing by starting at the ready position (elbow at shoulder level and up, forearm and racket pointing straight up). Think of the racket as a hammer and the ball as a nail. Toss the ball about two feet above the hammer, letting the racket head drop some behind the back, and then "throw" the racket forward and up to the ball using a pronounced wrist action such as in hammering a nail. The racket head falls down to the opposite side of your body at the finish.

The "Hammer-Nail" serve starts at the ready position.

**The Beginning Serve
Illustrated**

BEGINNING NET PLAY

Volley

Stand about six to eight feet from the net. The set position is the same as for the forehand and backhand drives, except that the racket head is at chest level. (The strike zone is now at chest level instead of waist level.) Keep your eyes on the ball and your head down; a top volleyer stays down and close to the ball, almost as if he is trying to catch it in his teeth.

On the *forehand* reach directly forward to the ball (no backswing unless the ball is very high) with the wrist laid back and with the racket as nearly parallel to the court as comfortably possible. Step across to the ball with the left foot, facing the point of contact with your shoulders. (Do not pivot your body, for this will cause the racket to go too far back.) Meet the ball flat with a firm wrist well in front of your body. Use an abrupt punching motion from the elbow, with little follow-through.

Forehand volley

On the *backhand* change to the backhand grip by bringing the right hand up to the level of the left hand, so that the racket is essentially parallel to the court in front of your chest. Step across to the ball with the right foot, and face the expected point of contact with your shoulders. (The left hand on the racket throat helps to keep you facing the ball and limits any backswing by helping you to keep the racket in front of your body.) The abrupt punching motion from the elbow causes the racket to move forward out of the left hand. The ball is hit flat.

Common Faults

1. *Too much swing is used.*
2. *The ball is contacted too late (not far enough in front).*
3. *The wrist fails to remain firm on contact.*
4. *The player fails to get close enough (body and eyes) to the ball.*
5. *The ball is slapped at from the wrist or is swung at from the shoulder. (It should be punched from the elbow).*

Backhand volley

Volley for a low ball

Overhead smash

For *low balls* lower the racket head to a point slightly below the level of the wrist. Keep the wrist firm on contact, and lift the ball softly up with some follow-through (instead of punching the ball abruptly).

Overhead Smash

If you are at the net and a high lob is returned to you, you may have an opportunity to smash it down to your opponent. An overhead smash is best described as a modified serve with abbreviated motion—since often there is not much time to react. From your set position at the net, turn your side by stepping back and move to get directly under the ball. (If you were to miss, the ball would hit you on the forehead.)

Raise your racket to the hammer-nail serve position as soon as you turn your side to the net. Keep your racket elbow at shoulder level as you wait for the ball. If your elbow drops, your swing will lengthen unnecessarily and it will be difficult to time your stroke accurately. When you are ready to hit, shift your weight onto your front foot. (It is often difficult to get set for an overhead shot, and many advanced players maintain their balance and get added power by engaging in a scissors kick just as the ball is hit.)

Common Faults

1. *The player fails to move under the ball (most overheads are missed because of bad footwork).*
2. *The player overswings.*
3. *The eyes fail to watch the ball closely enough.*

Throw your racket and arm forward and up to the ball, contacting the ball as high above your head as possible. Watch the ball with extra care: there is a tendency with this shot to pull your head down and take your eyes off the ball just before it is hit. Use a pronounced wrist snap to smash the ball into your opponent's court. Follow through in the direction of the shot and then over to the opposite side of your body.

INTERMEDIATE AND ADVANCED STROKES

There is no magic point in your tennis development at which you should begin to learn more refined strokes. It may be several years before you have mastered the forehand and backhand drive, the serve, and the volley of the preceding sections and are ready to undertake the underspin shots and the advanced serves of this section. As a general guide, do not attempt too much at once. Lay a good foundation and then build slowly, adding only when each preceding block is anchored firmly in place.

Drop Shot

The drop shot is a soft underspin shot that falls into your opponent's court close to the net and does not bounce very high.

Use a short backswing, and hold the racket head open and above the wrist. The hit is softly down and under the ball. As the racket comes under the ball, open the racket face more so that the ball is given a slight up and forward lift. The racket finishes at eye level with the face still open.

Forehand drop shot

The drop shot, more than any other stroke, is a liability rather than an asset if played improperly. It is not usually an outright winner in top tennis; it is more of a tactical shot to pull your opponent out of position and to set up a following shot. The drop shot is most effective when sharply angled or hit behind your opponent. Use it only on short balls and on relatively unimportant points, to keep your opponent off balance.

Drop Volley

This is simply a soft volley hit with some underspin which, like the drop shot, causes the ball to "stop" after bouncing. The racket face opens and the wrist relaxes on contact with the ball. There is almost no backswing or follow-through.

Slice

The slice is an underspin shot that makes the ball "float" over the net and then bounce flat and low.

The racket passes down and through the ball at less than a 45-degree angle to put a backspin on the ball. The

Backhand drop volley

racket head must be above the wrist and the anticipated point of contact at the ready position. The racket face is slightly beveled upward or "open," and the backswing is short. The follow-through is down through the line of the shot and then up to shoulder level.

The slice is effective as a down-the-line approach shot to the net when taken at the top of the bounce inside the baseline, as a change of pace when hit from behind the baseline, or as a serve return when standing in close.

Chop

A chop is an underspin shot in which the ball "sits up" in the air and "stops" after the bounce.

The racket head at the ready position is considerably above the point of contact, and above waist level. The racket face is almost standing on edge, as compared to the open face of the slice, and the backswing is short. The racket passes down at the ball at slightly more than a 45-degree angle. There is little follow-through, since the motion is almost straight down.

A chop is best used by advanced players as a deep change of pace shot or as a drop shot to draw the opponent up to the net. However, because the chop shot demands perfect timing, it should be one of the last strokes learned.

Backhand slice

Forehand chop

Grip for spin serve

J Motion for topspin serve

Topspin Serve

All good servers hit mostly spin serves. The spin tends to slow the ball down and afford more net clearance, although the spin serve can be served very hard.

One of the most common spin serves is the topspin serve. As with other spin serves, this requires a grip tending more toward the backhand. In order to hit up across the back of the ball, you must throw the ball farther behind your front foot then you would for a flat serve. If the ball were to drop to the court, it would land in front of the forward heel.

The set position is the same as for the flat serve, but on the toss the body turns more sideways. This allows the tossing arm to be more above and parallel to the baseline, rather than pointing toward your opponent. The tossing arm thus makes a letter J in its motion, which allows the ball to be tossed in front of, but over, the shoulder.

The knees are bent with the weight on the front foot on the toss, but the front leg extends as the server reaches up for the ball. This causes the back foot to come forward and fall into the court on the finish.

The racket head drops behind the back, but instead of hitting forward flatly in the direction of the shot, the racket moves up to the ball in a line more parallel to the baseline; in other words, it hits up across the back of the ball from side to side. Think of "brushing" the back of the ball upwards with the edge of the hand.

In order to hit upward, you must let the ball drop some from the peak of the toss. The racket contacts the ball on the way down, and then extends all the way up with a pronounced wrist snap. To help you hit up, the side stays toward the net longer. After the toss, the tossing arm tucks in against the chest to help keep the shoulders from turning forward too soon. The finish is to the left side of the body.

American Twist Serve

This is the extreme version of the topspin serve. The server hits up on the ball, and kicks his wrist hard over the top of the ball, giving the ball a pronounced curve, resulting in a high reverse bounce.

Hitting angle—flat serve

The ball is thrown even further behind the body than on a topspin serve. This causes the body to bend more backwards to reach the ball, but makes it easier to hit up on the ball. A strong upward push from the front leg adds to the upward hitting action.

The hit is up and out from the inside corner of the ball, and then the wrist kicks the racket hard over the top of the ball. This "reverse" of the wrist is critical to the reverse bounce of the ball. The swing is at almost right angles to the direction of the hit.

The finish is to the left side of the body as the shoulders finally turn into the hit, and the back leg comes across the line.

Slice Serve

The slice serve is similar to the flat serve, except that the grip is more toward a backhand, and the ball is thrown to the right side of the body so the server can hit around the outside of the ball.

Hitting angle—slice serve

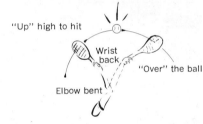

"Up" high to hit

Wrist back

"Over" the ball

Elbow bent

Wrist action—American Twist serve

Intermediate and Advanced Serves Illustrated

Slice serve

Topspin serve

Twist serve

PrINCIPLes
OF sINGLes straTeGY

The player with sound strokes is at a distinct advantage in a tennis match, but it is essential to realize that strokes are only a means to an end. Strokes enable you to make the best use of strategy, and once they are learned you must strive to use them as intelligently and as efficiently as possible to get the job done.

In order to master the strategy of a winning singles game you must progress through five areas of development:

> Keeping the Ball in Play
> Keeping the Ball Deep
> Moving Your Opponent
> Mounting the Attack
> Defending Against the Attack

The first three are concerned primarily with an application of ground strokes (forehand and backhand). The fourth requires an understanding of the net game, including approach shots, and the development of a more aggressive serve. Having mastered these tactics you will have progressed into strong intermediate or advanced play, your opponents also will be more aggressive, and you will be ready for the fifth area, how to defend against the attack.

KEEPING THE BALL IN PLAY

Assume Proper Court Position

You must know where to wait for your opponent's shot in order to be best able to return it. Each player stands one or two feet behind his baseline, approximately in the center of the court. Be careful not to get caught in "No Man's Land" (mid-court) unless you are purposely going to the net. Balls will bounce behind you or at your feet when you are in mid-court, and they are not

27

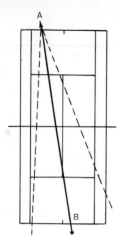

Set position
Bisects angle of return.

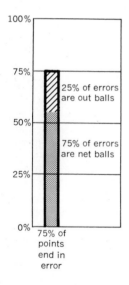

25% of errors
are out balls

75% of errors
are net balls

75% of
points
end in
error

Balance errors and placements.

only difficult shots to return, you will usually be forced to hit them up (defensively). If you have to run into No Man's Land for a short ball, return quickly to your home base behind the baseline, or go on to the net. Don't remain in No Man's Land.

Bisect the possible angle of return   Always return to a position behind the baseline that bisects the angle your opponent may hit to. For example, if the ball is being hit from Point A, you assume a set position at Point B, slightly to the right of the center mark.

Play Percentage Tennis

Make your opponent hit the ball   This is the first and foremost rule in tennis for the advanced as well as the beginning player. Concentrate on keeping the ball going back to your opponent. Don't let him off the hook by trying an unnecessary shot and missing or getting caught out of position. You need only hit the ball in court one more time than your opponent to win the point. And if you keep the ball in play, you apply pressure on your opponent to hit a placement to beat you.

Try to balance errors and placements   Seventy-five percent of all points are lost because of unnecessary errors—balls that could have been returned—whereas only 25% are lost because of placements—shots hit so well they could not have been returned. Of unnecessary errors, another three-quarters are because the ball hit the net, and only one-quarter because the ball landed out of bounds.

It is inevitable that you will make errors! Even in championship tennis it is a rarity to have a perfect balance of errors and placements. But play percentage tennis and cut down on *unnecessary* errors. The player who wins is the one who makes fewer errors—and who makes fewer of them at critical times. Don't try a $10 shot if a 10¢ will accomplish the same result. This is what separates the men from the boys in tennis, and why some people are better competitors than others.

Play each point   Point by point concentration puts tremendous pressure on your opponent. It is possible to lose more points than you win and still win the set. Know the critical points. All points are important but on certain points it is more essential that you not make a careless error. For instance, try to win the first point

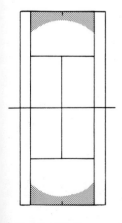

and get a jump on your opponent. The first games in each set are important too. Don't make the mistake of overhitting with risky shots early in the game or match, especially when playing any opponent you think is better than you.

The third point is crucial. It can keep you from falling decisively behind, or it can give you a commanding lead.

As the game nears a climax, apply all the concentration possible on every ball that is hit. Avoid needless errors at 40-30, deuce, or advantage. This is like the situation of a pitcher with a 3-2 count on the batter.

The seventh game is critical:

You		Opponent		7th		Score
5	+	1	+	1	=	6-1
4	+	2	+	1	=	5-2
3	+	3	+	1	=	4-3
2	+	4	+	1	=	3-4
1	+	5	+	1	=	2-5

At the set level, the seventh game is one of the most critical games. The score will be 5-1, 4-2, 3-all, 2-4, or 1-5. The winner of the seventh game will probably win the set, if he is ahead.

Practice Being Steady

As a beginner see how long you can rally, how many consecutive balls you can hit against a backboard or a steady partner. As a complete beginner, or if you are very young, rally in the serve square, since it forces you to hit softly (thereby developing touch, feel, and control), and gives you time to think about your strokes. Gradually move back to full court.

As a more advanced player, though you are hitting the ball to your opponent, try to "out-rally" him in the warm-up. Practice by playing points, and try to play as many points as possible without an error, both against a steady player and against an attacking player.

Play a "two more errors than placements" game. Play rally points, with every error you make counting as a "minus one" and every placement you make counting as a "plus one." If you commit two more errors than you make placements before your opponent does, you lose the game.

KEEPING THE BALL DEEP

As you play more, and encounter better players, you find that keeping the ball in play is not enough. You now must not only keep the ball safely in play, but also keep the ball deep.

Depth is important.

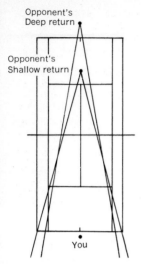

Opponent's
Deep return

Opponent's
Shallow return

You

A deep return reduces
hitting angle.

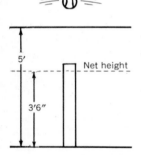

5'

Net height

3'6"

A beginner's floater shot
must clear the net by 5'-8'
for depth to result.

A deep ball is difficult to
handle.

A deep shot is a ball that lands near the rear boundary of the court. This shot makes it more difficult for your opponent to respond aggressively, since:

a) His hitting angle is reduced, giving you less court to cover;

b) His shot takes longer to get back to you (since it must travel further), giving you more time to prepare.

These two facts are important to remember when you are in trouble and out of position. A deep, floating ball gives you time to recover and prepare.

For the beginner who has not yet learned to hit the ball safely and with power a deep ball must clear the net by a good five to eight feet if it is being hit from near the baseline. A beginner hitting from a distance behind the baseline, may even have to hit a lob—a ball that clears the net by more than eight feet—to keep the shot deep. A more advanced player who hits with more power must only clear the net by two to three feet on most shots from the baseline. From substantially behind the baseline, though, he must hit a higher floating ball.

The deep floater ball bounces high and forces your beginning or intermediate opponent to move substantially back from the baseline to return the ball. This increases the chance of a weak return. For more advanced play, it has value also as a change of pace shot, and can be used to slow down a hard-hitting opponent.

Practice Depth

It may help you to realize how high the ball must clear the net to obtain depth if you attach a pole to each net post and connect them with a cord stretching about five feet above the top of the net. All balls must be hit over the cord.

For practice play rally points or "two more errors than placements" and count it as a miss any time the ball lands in front of the service line or in front of a taped line placed between the service line and the baseline.

MOVING YOUR OPPONENT

Keeping the ball in play and keeping it deep are essential and primary concepts, but they are basically defensive. You should, even at the beginning level, be combining these two principles with the third, and more aggressive, principle of singles strategy, that of moving your opponent.

From your very first introduction to the strokes of tennis, you have learned the importance of footwork, of trying to set and step into the direction of the hit. You know that this weight transfer helps control and power. You must also know by now that you do a lot of moving around the court, and that it is not always possible for you to set your feet and make a powerful and controlled return.

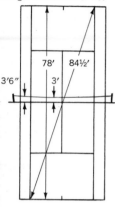

Longer court — lower net

Use a cross court shot for added safety.

You are ready now to attempt to do the same to your opponent—to run him from side to side, up and back, in order to create an opening or to force him to hit a weak shot. In other words, you should try to keep him from getting set, where he can direct his shots with power.

Move Your Opponent from Side to Side

There are two directions you can hit to move your opponent from side to side: diagonally across the court, or down the sideline. Each shot has its advantages.

Cross court shots   The cross court shot, which is almost always a topspin drive, fits well into the strategy you have learned so far. It is a safe beginning shot, because:

a) The ball must travel over the center of the net, which is six inches lower than it is at the sides.
b) The court is about six and a half feet longer diagonally from side to side than it is down the line.
c) Cross court shots give you more margin on a difficult surface or when playing in the wind. (A down-the-line return of a cross court shot will tend to ricochet wide off your racket.)
d) Keeping the ball deep is not so essential. Since a cross court shot often has sufficient angle to pull your opponent wide, it makes it impossible for him to get into position to attack.

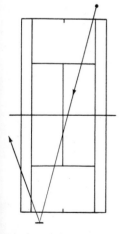

A ball coming cross court tends to ricochet wide off the racket.

Use a cross court shot:

a) To get your opponent moving. Start the point immediately with a cross court shot: it makes your opponent run more since it can be hit to greater angles. Even if you are hitting to his strength, a cross court shot will help to expose his weakness on the next shot.

Use a cross court shot when out of position.

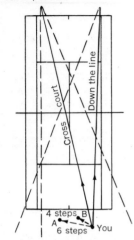

Set position bisects possible angle of return. On a down the line shot, recover to point A. Cross court, recover to point B.

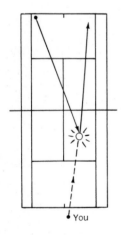

Move in quickly and hit forcefully down the line often when ball is returned short.

b) If your opponent hits down the line to you. He will have to move a considerable distance to reach the ball. This gives you an excellent chance to win the point outright.

c) When you are on the defensive. You don't have so far to recover in order to bisect the possible angle of return.

Down the line shots A down the line shot is often an underspin shot, such as a slice or chop, and should be used:

a) As a change in routine to the basic cross court pattern.

b) To help get at a player's weakness.

c) To hit behind a person running fast to cover the opposite side of the court.

d) As the basic attack shot (described in the next sequence).

Allow more margin for error on a down the line shot. Use considerable spin and aim well inside the sideline, since:

a) The ball travels a shorter distance and over a higher part of the net.

b) It is more difficult to follow through the flight of the ball, so the ball tends to slide off the racket to the side.

Move Your Opponent Up and Back

Basically you want to keep your opponent as far in the back court as possible. However, many players don't move forward as well as they move to the side. Also, some players stay in the back court because they feel insecure at the net. If your opponent never moves up to the net, float a few balls high and deep. If he retreats back to return and his return lands at all short, hit softly and short yourself (a drop shot, for instance) to force him to come to the net. Once he gets to the net, be certain to lob often to him, for he may not be coming to the net because of an overhead weakness.

You may also want to return short because your opponent is pulling you to the net and then successfully lobbing or passing you. If you are not effective when you are inadvertently pulled to the net, pull your opponent up by using a soft, short shot (drop shot) instead of an approach shot. Even if they don't pull your opponent all the way to the net, short underspin shots following high floaters can be effective change of pace shots.

(Hit only down the line)

B

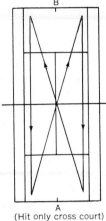

A

(Hit only cross court)

Three ways to play a short ball.

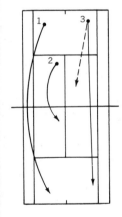

1. A defensive floater, allowing time to retreat to the baseline.

2. A drop shot to pull your opponent up.

3. A hard drive as the first shot in the attack to the net.

Practice Moving Your Opponent

Play points from the baseline to learn the value of cross court shots, down the line shots, hard topspin drives, soft high floaters, underspins, and drop shots. Work on setting and balancing by using a cross court-down the line drill: Player A hits only cross court; Player B hits only down the line. Emphasize depth, especially on the down the line shots (make all balls land behind the serve line). The value of the game is lost if you try to hit too hard (¾ speed is ample), if you play the ball so close to the line that shots are needlessly missed, or if you are careless about setting.

MOUNTING THE ATTACK

So far, we have discussed mostly defensive tennis. And we have seen how basically defensive maneuvers (deep balls or balls which move your opponent) can force your opponent to make weak or inaccurate returns. We will now explore the considerations involved in taking the offensive in play and during service.

When a short ball is hit to you and you are forced to move into the playing court to return it, you may:

a) Play it 100% defensively by returning it fairly softly, high, and deep, and down the middle—giving your opponent no angle for return and giving yourself time to retreat to a more comfortable position behind the baseline.

b) Play it somewhat defensively by returning it as a drop shot, which tends to pull your opponent up out of position into No Man's Land and gives you time to recover, either back to the baseline or occasionally to the net.

c) Play it 100% offensively and "mount the attack" by approaching the net.

We have already discussed the first two. Now we will learn *how* and *when* to mount the attack and approach the net with a ground stroke.

Approach the Net on a Ground Stroke

Intermediate and even advanced beginning players can have reasonable success playing at the net (we have seen how mechanically simple the volley really is) provided they come to the net at the right time with the right shot. In other words, the most critical factor of

successful net play is the method of getting there—the approach itself.

When to approach the net   The approach to the net should be attempted on any ball that bounces near the serve line (unless it is sharply angled), provided you can be balanced and set in position at the net when the opponent returns. It is wise to approach the net often when playing with a strong wind at your back, since your opponent will have to return into the wind. Don't approach the net on a ball that bounces near your baseline, as you will probably not be able to get close enough to the net to make your first volley effective.

Anticipation of the short ball helps to make your approach shot easier. You must learn to "feel" when the return may be short (a result of a deep or hard shot, or because the opponent had to run a great distance), and be mentally prepared to move in quickly. Anticipation will get you started a split second sooner, and will allow you time to get to the ball and be balanced and set. (Hopefully your opponent will help you by being somewhat out of position for his return of your approach shot.)

How to approach the net   ,An inexperienced player will probably come to the net only when chasing up for a very short ball—when his momentum carries him so far forward he can't retreat. A more advanced player will try to set up a short return from his opponent, especially to his forehand, so he can attack the net.

Remember, you have worked the entire rally to get this opportunity. From more steady play, your thoughts must be immediately changed to "attack"—like the tiger who has worked himself in position to finally "make his kill." At the same time, don't get careless when you finally have the opportunity to attack. Don't overhit. Unless you have an obvious opening, be content to use the approach shot as an interim shot to set up the winning volley. Give yourself plenty of margin.

Follow the ball to the net. This will help you to bisect the possible angle of return and thus to best cover the return. If the return is coming from substantially behind the baseline, your opponent must lob, so don't get quite so close to the net. Also, if your opponent is hitting from behind the baseline, his cross court angle is very limited.

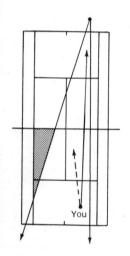

Cover the down-the-line passing shot. Give your opponent the short cross court angle (shaded).

"split"

Hop to a "split" stop as your opponent contacts the ball.

"Split" to a balanced stop. Hop up so that you land momentarily with both feet split apart on the ground as your opponent contacts the ball. It is important to be completely set when your opponent contacts the ball; don't get caught running headlong forward in an effort to get all the way to the net. Don't come to the net on a ground stroke unless you feel you can get far enough in to cut down effective angle returns and low balls. Be able to change direction by having good balance.

How to hit the approach shot   Hit the ball early on the approach. Try to contact the ball no later than the top of the bounce. This gives your opponent less time to prepare.

The earlier the ball is met and the closer to the net you are, the shorter the swing. Most balls taken "on the rise" are hit with underspin, since it requires less backswing and is easier to time, and since the underspin ball tends to bounce low and skid, which forces your opponent to hit up.

Depth is important on your approach shot.

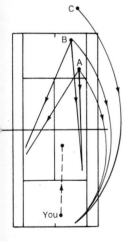

Player A has three good chances to pass you.

Player B has a reasonable chance to pass you.

Player C can probably only lob.

Where to hit the approach shot   A more advanced player will usually hit down the line on his approach, since he recognizes that a down the line approach:
a) Cuts down the court area he must cover on the return. (Cover the down the line passing shot first; almost give your opponent the short cross court angle.)
b) Makes it easier to get into position for the volley, since he only has to move straight ahead to cover the down the line return.

You should concentrate on depth more than speed in your approach shot (unless you have a clear-cut opportunity for a winner), since this limits what your opponent may do on his return. Try to keep your return to your opponent's backhand, unless you have a big opening on the forehand side. A premium must be placed on keeping the approach deep, since a deep shot increases the possibility of a lob or a down the line return.

(A short ball makes it much easier for the opponent to hit the short cross court angle.) It is relatively simple to cover two possibilities, but almost impossible to cover three.

How to react to the return   After "splitting," move to the ball and make your shot. (Many times only one step

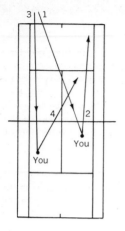

If the ball is returned cross court (1), volley down the line (2).

If the ball is returned down the line (3), volley cross court (4).

Use a slice serve to get the ball wide to the forehand.

will be needed.) Hit for the opening. If the ball is returned down the line, volley cross court. If the ball is returned cross court, volley down the line. If the ball is low, the volley must be deep or very sharply angled. Take the ball as early as possible so it doesn't have time to drop below the level of the net. If the ball is lobbed very high, let it bounce before hitting for better timing. Otherwise always hit it on the fly. (Sun and wind may be a factor in letting the ball bounce.) Hit the overhead aggressively from the forecourt (it is the most effective shot in tennis), and play it more defensively (less swing and power; use some spin) when hitting from deeper in the back court.

Use the Serve as an Offensive Weapon

As a beginner and advanced beginner you have probably been primarily concerned with getting the ball in play and maybe to your opponent's backhand. As you gain more confidence you use more variety on your serve (speed, spin, placement), and start to use the serve to offensive advantage.

Make your first serves   Your philosophy as a server should be to try to get at least two-thirds of your first serves in the court. Don't waste your first serve just because you are entitled to another. You can serve more aggressively (and yet competitively) on your first serve just because you have another chance. Remember that if you miss your first serve, it is just like the pitcher falling behind the batter. There is much less opportunity to take the offense. The receiver knows this and will play accordingly.

On important points, however, when it is important to keep the pressure on your opponent, a much higher percentage of first serves must be good, even if it means serving less aggressively. If you are substantially behind, you might as well serve more aggressively and try to get back in the game quickly. Above all, don't double fault. It is just like walking the batter. If it occurs at ad out, it is just like walking in a run.

Mix up your serves   A hard flat serve to the backhand may be your most effective serve but you can't use it all the time, any more than a pitcher would use only a fast ball. Keep your opponent guessing and off balance.

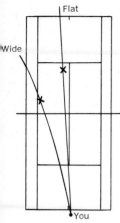

Serve wide to pull your
opponent out of position.

Serve *wide* to your opponent if:

a) You have a natural angle, such as a slice to the fore-hand in the forehand court or a twist to the back-hand in the backhand court.

b) Your opponent undercuts (slices) most returns. This may mean he can't return well with a drive—the natural return for a wide ball, especially when hitting cross court.

c) Your opponent assumes a faulty set position—too far behind the baseline, or too far to one side of the court.

d) Your opponent backs up on a wide serve instead of stepping in and cutting off the angle.

e) Your opponent moves in to return in an attempt to come directly to the net. A wide serve tends to pull him off the court and makes it more difficult for him to get to the net.

f) There is a concentration let-down (after a long point or a long game). This is a good time for a wide serve to the forehand.

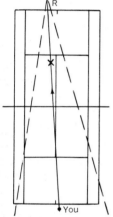

Serve flat down the middle to
cut down angle on the return.

Serve *tight* into your opponent (for example, to his fore-hand in the ad court) if:

a) He normally takes a big swing on his return. A ball close to his body makes a big swing difficult.

b) He is hurting you with angle returns. Don't give him the angle.

Serve *high* (topspins or twists) to your opponent if:

a) He can't return a high ball well. Many players can't hit through a high ball well.

Serve *deep* to your opponent if:

a) You want to significantly cut down the effectiveness of his return, especially on second serves where he may be moving in to get more angle. (If you are having trouble serving with depth, throw the ball more forward and hit with less spin.)

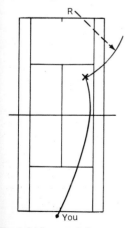

The twist is a good change
of pace serve.

Vary your pace   Some receivers rely on the pace of the serve for the effectiveness of their return. Don't hesitate to use more spin and slow the ball down occasionally, even on a first serve. When you serve a hard flat serve, remember the net is lowest in the center and that the ball gets to the receiver sooner down the middle than when it is hit wide. (The ball will be coming back quickly as well, but with little angle for the return.)

Use your head in deciding when to come to the net on your serve.

The server poised for power. Don't come to the net on a weak serve.

Attack the Net on the Serve

When to come to the net behind the serve   Obviously, a beginner will rarely use the serve as an attacking weapon. The intermediate player may occasionally come to the net on a first serve, but rarely on the second serve. An advanced player may come to the net on both the first and second serves as a standard play, especially on faster hard courts and grass, or when serving with the wind at his back.

Don't come to the net if you are uncertain about hitting a strong serve. Your opponent can readily exploit your vulnerable position and either pass you outright or force a very weak volley. (A weak serve is made even more ineffective on a slow court such as rough cement or clay, or when serving into a strong wind. In these conditions place less emphasis on attack, especially on a second serve.)

You may stay back on the serve if you have been regularly unsuccessful using the serve as an attacking shot, (perhaps your opponent has too good a return, or you have been missing many first serves) or to see if your opponent is steady enough to play well in backcourt rallies. You may stay back in a particular game on your serve (and yet perhaps come in on the first short ball, even the return) if you find yourself down 0-30, 0-40, or 15-40, as a change of pace and to help break your opponent's rhythm.

In any case, you must make up your mind either to go to the net or stay back before you serve. You must not wait to see whether the serve is good or effective.

How to come to the net behind the serve   The back foot comes across the baseline into the court on the follow-through of the serve as the first step in getting to the net. Move forward as rapidly as possible, jumping to a "split" stop at the instant your opponent contacts the return ball. On a slow serve you will have more time to get closer to the net. Get as close to the net as quickly as possible, commensurate with being completely balanced and set on contact with the return. (Players who don't set well are especially susceptible to hard returns driven low, tending to run by the ball.) You should have time for three or four steps before coming to your "split" stop. This puts you in the vicinity of the serve line, although probably slightly behind it. You must accept

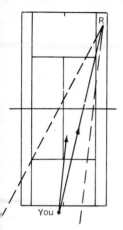

When going to the net as a server, assume a set position that bisects the possible angle of return.

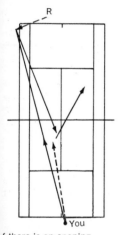

If there is an opening, volley to it.

Net advance drill.

Four hit overhead drill.

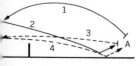

the fact that it is impossible to get all the way to the net from behind the baseline before the ball is returned. Thus, you will have to hit one "approach" shot (volley) from the difficult and relatively vulnerable area of No Man's Land.

After your "split" stop, move forward to the ball where you want to contact it. Set again for the volley and try to contact the ball in front of the serve line. Since you are not yet close enough to put much angle on your return, the premium on this shot is depth. Now follow the ball to the net, as when approaching on a ground stroke. Treat the first volley as an approach shot—don't overhit the ball. The first volley should set up your second volley.

If there is an opening volley to it. (For example, a wide serve to the backhand in the backhand (ad) court, especially if the ball is returned down the line, leaves the forehand court open.) It there is no obvious opening, play the shot conservatively. In fact, many good players volley essentially down the middle of the court in order to cut down the angle for the passing shot.

Practice Attacking to the Net

Approaching off the ground stroke   Use a back court rally and come in on the first short ball. Either play points or play "two more errors than placements." A variation is to start the rally by hitting short to Player B. Player B hits the approach and comes to the net for the volley. Player A tries to pass.

Approaching off the serve   Players A and B serve and volley to Player C, who returns. Play points, "two more errors than placements," or simply see who can go longest without an error.

Practicing net play   Both players start at the baseline, and both work their way to the net slowly after each hit. Keep all balls down the middle at ¾ speed. Once the net is reached, keep a volley rally going. This drill gives you much practice on low and half volleys.

An alternative is "four-hit": Player A alternates drives and lobs, which gives Player B (at the net) volley and overhead practice. All balls should be hit down the middle of the court at ¾ speed.

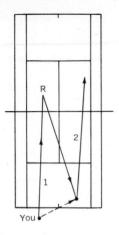

When passing: use the first shot (1) to pull your opponent out of position so you can pass him on the second shot (2).

Don't panic against a net rusher. Use many lobs to tie the net man up.

DEFENSE AGAINST THE ATTACK

Most important in defending against the attack, don't be pressed into trying too good a shot against the net rusher. Don't feel you have only one shot in which to win the point. Make your opponent hit the ball to beat you. The fact that he is at the net doesn't mean he wins the point automatically: it is remarkable how many "sure" winners are missed at the net. Unless you are confident of hitting an outright winner, use the first shot to pull your opponent out of position, and then be more aggressive on the second shot. Take your time. Don't be rushed into not setting or staying down with your shot.

Use Lobs

The lob is probably the most under-used shot in tennis. Occasionally on short balls, especially on down the middle balls where little passing angle exists, a quick lob can be effective and actually almost an offensive weapon. Give yourself plenty of margin (never miss a lob wide), and get the ball well up into the air. Anytime you are successful in getting the lob over the net player's head, move into the net yourself. Even if the lob doesn't get over the net player's head, it tends to push him away from the net, and makes passing shots easier.

Lob always when hitting from substantially behind the baseline. Lob often if the sun is a factor, even when not hitting from so deep in the back court. Although it is difficult to lob in the wind, it is even more difficult to hit an overhead in the wind. (Don't lob as high when hitting with the wind.) On hot days lob extensively early in the match. If the match turns out to be a long one, this could be the determining factor.

Use Passing Shots

The most important principle in using passing shots is to keep the ball low, so that if the volleyer reaches it, he will be forced to hit up, thus decreasing his opportunity to make an aggressive return shot. Topspin balls drop faster than flat or underspin shots. Therefore, most passing shots are hit with substantial topspin.

Down the line The most common passing drives are hit down the line. The ball gets to the opponent sooner

"Home base" for the receiver.

Return of serve

on a down the line shot, and gives him less time to prepare. Also, it is difficult for a net player running to the side to get the racket around the ball fast enough to hit cross court.

Since the net player is probably covering the down the line shot, you must hit the ball fairly hard to get by him. Recover quickly after the shot, since the net player will try to volley to the cross court opening.

Cross court   The cross court passing shot is a good shot if you have the opportunity to hit it, especially when the ball has been volleyed short and low. It is not as important to hit the ball hard, and indeed if your shot is low and soft, there is very little the volleyer can do. And by keeping your ball cross court, your opponent has less opening to volley to—leaving you less area to cover in reaching the next shot.

Many times the soft "change of pace" shot will pull your opponent far enough out of position to set up the passing shot on the next hit, or will pull him close to the net and make him vulnerable to the lob.

Return Against the Server

A good server has the initial advantage whether or not he comes to the net behind his serve. However, a good return can at least neutralize the advantage of the server.

Assume proper court position   If you begin in the correct position, you may not have to move at all to return the serve, especially when standing in close to cut down the angles. As receiver, your "home base" is on the baseline and about one foot from the alley. This position is adjusted, depending on where the server stands—as for any shot, you should be in a line that bisects the possible angle of serve—and how hard he serves. Stand back a little behind the baseline if your opponent is a hard server, or somewhat inside the baseline if he is a soft server.

A simple shoulder turn and a straight, short backswing instead of a full step and pivot may be all that is needed to get the racket back if you are in the right position. Think of the return in two parts: 1) turn the shoulders and take the racket back (don't step across your body), 2) step into the hit on the forward swing.

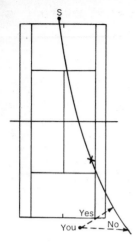

Don't let a wide serve drive you back.

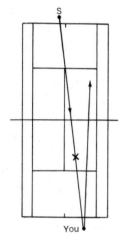

Basic return against a net rusher.

If you have to move wide to hit the return, move forward and wide, to cut down the angle of the serve. Don't let a wide serve drive you back. Likewise, don't charge the ball. A common beginner's mistake is to run forward into the ball instead of turning. Stay down with the ball —the knees always bend on returns. Don't rise up upon contact.

Neutralize the net rusher's advantage   Concentration helps you to be mentally ready—"keyed"—for each serve, and helps you to watch the ball. It helps you see the coming serve as a challenge, and it also challenges the server to give you a good serve. Don't let a server who rushes the net press you into trying to hit too good a return (unless it is an obvious winner). The basic return against a net rusher is a regular topspin or a fairly flat drive slightly to your opponent's backhand, but essentially down the middle and low. There is less chance of your missing this return, and you give the volleyer little angle. Ideally, your return will be low to make the volleyer hit up.

Vary your returns   Many net rushers like to volley a hard return, but get all tied up when the return comes soft. Use a soft, unspectacular underspin chip return often, especially against a hard hitter, or an extremely fast net rusher.

Above all, if you are unsuccessful returning one way, change and try something different—standing in closer or back farther, hitting softer or harder, hitting for more angle or less angle, or moving in yourself.

Shorten your backswing and move in some on the return when your opponent is having difficulty serving (especially on short second serves) and you think you can pressure him. Also move in when your opponent is getting too close to the net for his first volley. You can keep him from getting in so close if you take the ball sooner yourself. Perhaps you can even beat him to the net by using the return as an approach shot.

Stand back farther than usual if you want more time to react. This also may upset a server's timing as he comes in. Keep the ball down the middle to minimize the chance for an angle volley, and be prepared to lob the second shot.

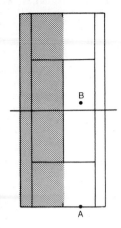

B
•

A

Up-back drill.

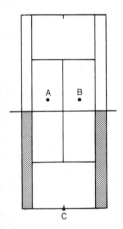

A   B
•   •

C

Aussie two-on-one.

Practice Against the Attacker

Play points against a net rusher, using one of the following drills.

Three on one ground stroke approach drill   Players A, B, and C on one side of the net alternate starting the rally from the baseline by hitting approach shots and following in to the net. Player D on the other side tries to pass.

Two on one serve and volley drill   Players A and B on one side serve and volley; player C returns and passes. The server should volley to the open area of the court.

Up-back drill   Use one half of the court, from the center line to the alley. Player A stands at the baseline and Player B at the net on the other side. Player A tries to pass Player B in every possible way—lobs, drives, soft balls, hard balls, and so on. (If A lobs the ball over B's head, Player A moves to the net to take the offensive.)

Australian "two on one" drill   Players A and B are at the net and are responsible for the entire court, including the alley. Player C is at the baseline on the other side, and covers only the singles court. Players A and B run Player C as much as possible without hitting outright winners. (Player C should just be able to get every ball.) Player C tries to win each point by attempting passing shots (drives and lobs).

Principles
of Doubles Strategy

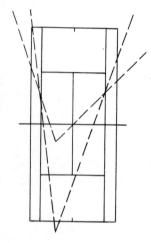

Basic principle: When at net you can hit to greater angles.

Once at the net you can hit down.

Doubles is an exciting and fast-moving game that requires great teamwork and communication between partners. You should keep this in mind in choosing a partner, and you should also give consideration to choosing a partner whose style of play might effectively complement your own playing style. (Often a quick touch player and a slower but more powerful partner form a good team.)

Even though the court is nine feet wider than in singles, both partners can cover the entire doubles court with comparative ease. Unlike singles, then, the probability is low that you will be able to maneuver your opponents out of position when you are hitting from the back court: the angle to which to hit is just too limited. It is also unlikely you will be able to use power as effectively from the back court—it is difficult to hit "through" two opponents from a back court position.

These two considerations dictate the basic doubles strategy: at the intermediate or advanced levels get to the net where angles do exist and where quickness and touch can do some good. Since the court is easier to cover, both partners can get to the net with less risk than in singles. Even in beginning doubles you and your partner should attempt to position yourselves at the net. Both the server's partner and the receiver's partner begin the point at the net, and both the server and the receiver should attempt to join their partners there as soon as possible. Once at the net, the prime goal is to make your opponents hit up to you so that you can move in and hit down.

Proper court position is the most important factor in successful doubles at the beginning level at least through the intermediate level. Basic positions and corresponding goals are now outlined, and then the more specific goals of each team in specific situations will be discussed.

BASIC COURT POSITIONS AND STRATEGY

Serving Positions

The server stands against the baseline between the alley and the center mark. The server's partner stands at least two feet from the alley and about ten feet from the net (closer in more advanced doubles). Usually the best server should serve first in each set. Sometimes a playing condition such as a tailwind or sun glare will favor beginning with the weaker server. (Neither server should have to serve into the sun if one is left-handed and the other right-handed.)

Positions for server and server's partner.

Positions for receiver and receiver's partner.

Receiving Positions

The receiver stands on the baseline at a point bisecting the angle where the ball may be served. The receiver's partner starts on the middle of the service line on his side of the court.

In determining who receives the first serve (which partner receives on the deuce court and which on the ad court) the prime consideration should be where each receiver feels more comfortable. Usually a player with a natural underspin backhand will play the deuce (forehand) court, where most serves are in close to the receiver's backhand. The partner with the better drive backhand (topspin) will usually play the ad (backhand) court, since there is more room on this side for a fuller return swing.

A left-handed player may play the backhand court to keep the server serving down the middle, and to keep both partners' forehands on the outside where more reach is needed. Or the left-hander may play the deuce court to keep both forehands in the middle where most balls are hit.

The stronger player may play the deuce court since more points (at least half) are served there (the ad receiver returns one less point in a 40-15 game, for example). Or the stronger player may play the ad court since he is better able to handle the pressure at "game point."

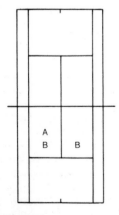

Beginning doubles rally position.

Net position

A: When one partner is at net (10' away).

B: When both are at net (15' away to help cover lob).

STRATEGY FOR THE BEGINNING SERVING TEAM

The Server

The beginner's serve will not be strong enough for the server to come to the net behind it. Therefore the beginner will only join his partner at the net if the ball is returned so short he must run up into the forecourt to hit. If you are a beginning server, remember some basic rules:

a) Try to serve as much as possible to your opponent's backhand.
b) Once the rally begins, use high cross court floaters to keep the ball away from the net man and to keep your opponent deep in the back court. After a couple of cross court exchanges, try to lob over the net player. This makes the receiver run more for the high, bouncing return. It means also that your partner at the net will have a good chance to intercept ("poach") the return.
c) If you are pulled up to the net to return a short ball, stay toward the rear of the service court. Don't get any closer than 15 feet from the net so you can protect against the lob.
d) Never remain in No Man's Land after moving up for a short ball. Preferably join your partner at the net; if you can't, retreat to a position behind the service line.

The Server's Partner

If you are the server's partner, stand at least two feet from the alley and about ten feet from the net. From that spot you can anticipate where the ball will be returned.

Your primary responsibility is to guard the alley, especially on balls served wide. However, when the ball bounces high and deep and in the center of the opponent's court, move slightly to the center of your court, away from the alley. (It is just about impossible that the ball will be returned to your alley, and by moving toward the center you have a good chance to poach the return.)

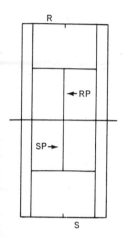

If the ball goes inadvertently to the opposing net player, back up a few feet and move toward the center of the court. This increases your chance to react to the ball—which will probably be directed either at your feet or between you and your partner.

If the ball is lobbed over your head, switch sides with your partner and let him take the shot. Drop back a few feet to just in front of the service line, in case your opponent poaches.

Once the rally begins, the net players should be alert for balls coming to the center of the court.

STRATEGY FOR THE INTERMEDIATE OR ADVANCED SERVING TEAM

Fewer chances should be taken with the first serve in doubles, and more margin should be allowed (more spin, for example) to get the ball in play. A good first serve is of great importance, since:

a) Your partner at the net can poach more effectively.

b) As server you can come to the net more readily. (An intermediate player should come to the net on many first serves, but much less often on second serves. An advanced player will come to the net regularly on both serves, since the majority of points will be won by the team that first gets to the net.)

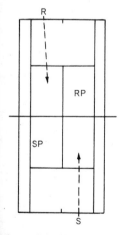

c) You have the strategic advantage. If you miss on the first serve, it will probably be easier for the receiver to return your second serve. You will usually hit your second serve with less pace and more spin which gives it a greater tendency to land short. Also you can take fewer chances on a second serve. The receiver knows it will almost always be served to his backhand, and he can gamble—run around his backhand, move in quicker, and so on.

Advanced doubles rally position.

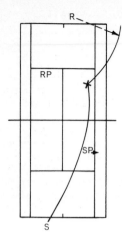

A wide serve slows down an attacking receiver.

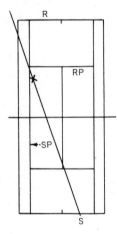

Server's partner moves with the ball.

Serve Wide

The most effective wide serves are the slice to the forehand of the deuce court and the twist to the backhand of the ad court. The wide serve can be effective if:

a) Your opponent is getting to the net off the return too quickly. A wide serve slows him down by moving him wide for the return instead of letting him move forward.

b) Your opponent has trouble returning a wide shot.

c) Both opponents are back behind the baseline. It tends to pull the receiver wide, which can open up the court for a poach by the server's partner.

Serve to the Middle

The serve to the middle of the court is the basic serve to the backhand of the deuce court. It is an effective serve to the ad court when:

a) Your opponent is "keying" for the usual serve to his backhand, especially on an "ad" point.

b) Your opponent overswings regularly on his forehand return. This ball can be served in tight to cramp his swing.

c) The receiver has a good angle return. This cuts down his return angle.

The ball served to the center of the court makes it easier for the server's partner to poach toward the center, since it is more difficult for the opponent to return the angle to the alley. For this reason the server's partner at the net will often begin the point standing closer to the center of the court in the deuce court,

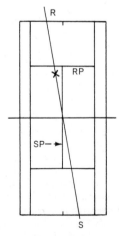

The serve down the middle makes it easier for the server's partner to poach.

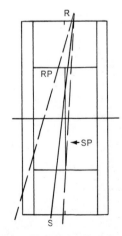

The serve down the middle gives the receiver less room to return.

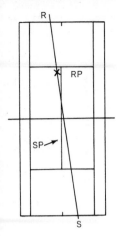

In poach, server's partner moves to center and server covers his partner's side.

since the basic serve is to the backhand (middle of the court). In the ad court the serve will more probably be wide, so the partner will often stand closer to the alley.

Poach

Poaching is a service strategy in which the net player moves toward his partner's side of the court to intercept the return shot. The poaching net player aims his return shot at the opening between the receiver who is back and the net player, or slightly toward the net player's feet. If the poaching player's momentum carries him to the server's side of the court, the serving partner moves to cover the poacher's original side.

If the serving team decides to poach often in a particular match, it may be advantageous for the net player to signal his intentions in advance to his partner. He might signal either a stay, a poach, or a fake poach. The decision to poach now becomes an all-or-nothing commitment. The server must cover his partner's side immediately upon serving.

If you are the server in a poaching situation, serve from a position closer to the center of the court. In order to protect against the angle return, serve more down the middle. The poach has the best chance to be effective on the first serve, so concentrate on getting the first serve in and don't try a risky serve.

The poach is a good move:
a) If you are having trouble winning the point serving to a particular side of the court. The poach can help break the receiver's rhythm and keep him from grooving his return. The receiver has many more things to think about against a poaching net player.
b) On a big point such as "ad out." The poach can help the server get out of a jam, especially if he has had to struggle to win serve.

Play "Australian Doubles"

Another service strategy to try to counteract an effective return (specifically, the wide angle return on the backhand from the ad court) is to position the server's partner on the same side of the court as the server, where he can intercept the cross court return. The server must serve from close to the center of the court so he can move over to the opposite side to cover the territory

Australian doubles positions

usually covered by his partner. If the server is serving to the ad court, the net player starts at the net on the left (instead of the right) side of the court. The server serves from the left side near the center, and then moves to the right side to continue the point. This forces the receiver to return down the line, often a difficult return for the player with a good cross court backhand. The maneuver may be tried on certain points to break the receiver's rhythm or to help get out of a particular jam.

STRATEGY FOR THE BEGINNING RECEIVING TEAM

The Receiver

The receiver attempts to keep the return away from the net player, and tries to hit it high and deep to the server. The rally continues with high, deep and floating shots being hit over the net back and forth between the server and receiver. If you are the beginning receiver, occasionally try to hit a lob over the net player. If the ball lands short, move in to return it and stay at the net with your partner.

The Receiver's Partner

The receiver's partner always watches his partner return the serve, and helps him call the service line. As soon as the receiver's partner sees that the return will not be intercepted by the net player, he moves up from the service line to his "home base" position about ten feet from the net. If his partner joins him at the net, both players remain about 15 feet from the net, to be better able to react to the impending lob situation. They now play side by side. If one partner must run back to retrieve a lob, his partner goes back too. (It is risky to stay at the net, since the retriever must probably lob, and the opponents will be moving in.) If both players are back and one partner moves up to hit, his partner moves up with him.

STRATEGY FOR THE INTERMEDIATE OR ADVANCED RECEIVING TEAM

The Receiver

A good return of serve is one of the most important shots in doubles, for it sets the tempo of the point. At the intermediate level the server may stay back, especially on the second serve. If you are the receiver, return the

Court positions if ball is lobbed over server's partner's head.

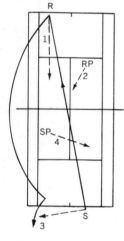

1. Receiver comes to net (not too close).

2. Receiver's partner moves in and covers the center.

3. Server moves over to take lob after it bounces (if he were coming to the net behind his serve, this is still his shot if it gets over his partner's head).

4. Server's partner crosses to the other side as soon as he sees he can't hit the lob. He covers the center and drops back in the service court in case his partner hits a bad shot.

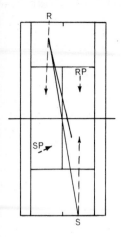

Low return; all four players move in.

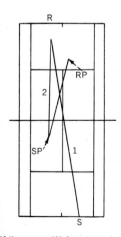

If the serve (1) is returned to the net player (2), the receiver's partner drops back and to the center to cover the volley (3).

ball high above the net and deep, away from the net player, as in beginning doubles. As receiver you should come to the net often on the return of serve.

In advanced doubles, the receiver assumes the server is coming to the net, and his goal is to keep the ball low to the approaching server in order to make him volley up. The receiver will also usually come to the net on the return of serve, although the first rule is to get the ball in play.

As an advanced receiver, adjust your court position so that you have the best chance to get the ball in play. Move back a little if you are having difficulty returning a hard serve. The farther back you stand, the more you can swing and drive the return (more topspin). The closer in you stand, the more you must shorten your swing and block or chip the return (more underspin). This also gives you a better chance to protect against the poach, to hit down on the return, and move in to volley.

Return more aggressively if you are substantially behind in a particular game. If the server's partner poaches often and effectively, a quick lob over the net player's head is a good play. Other possibilities are to try to pass down the alley, or to start the point with both partners at the baseline.

The Receiver's Partner

If you are the receiver's partner, you normally begin on the center of the service line. Your responsibility is to call out serves and watch your partner's return. If the return is reasonably low and to the approaching server, move forward to a position about ten feet from the net. If the return goes toward the net player (either because of a poor return or a poach), move back and toward the center to give yourself time to react and to cut off the opening in the middle of the court. If the return of serve is low and to the center of the court, you can poach to the center.

As the receiver's partner, you may choose to stand back at the baseline if:

a) The server's partner is poaching often (on first serves, for example) and effectively. The poacher is less able to hit an outright winner at your feet or between partners if you are back.

When receiving team stays back, keep balls in center of court and lob often.

b) Your partner is having particular trouble on his return. With both partners back, the receiver has more margin on his return—the low return is not so critical. The receiver can concentrate on just getting the ball back.

c) The server is consistently beating the receiver to the net, and by better positioning is winning the point on his first volley. Both of you should stay back. Play from the back court not only requires a less exacting return, but makes it more difficult for the opposing server to put the first volley away for a winner.

d) The serving team is a *groove* team and has established a fast pace and momentum. The receiving team should stay back to try to break the momentum. This can also be effective as a psychological maneuver on select points, such as the first couple of points of the game if the serving team has been holding serve rather easily through the first part of the set.

e) You want to exploit an opponent's weak overhead. In this situation the receiver and his partner stand substantially back and just try to get the ball in play on the return. Once it is in play, lob high and often, mixing in short, low drives.

When you elect to stay back, most balls should be hit down the middle to avoid giving your opponents the angle. (If one opponent is farther away from the net, hit the drive to him.) If the lob gets over your opponent's head, move in with your partner. Most important, be patient and keep the ball in play. Make your opponents work hard and hit a lot of balls to win the point.

STRATEGY WHEN BOTH TEAMS ARE AT THE NET

The great majority (75%) of all points in advanced doubles end with all four players at the net, like infighting in boxing. While waiting for an offensive opportunity, the emphasis is on keeping the ball low. This often requires a softer shot. Once the ball is hit up, however, the opposing team moves in for the knockout punch.

Down the Middle Balls

Most balls are hit down the middle when all four players are at the net. If you are moving in when a ball is returned down the middle, you should probably take the

Players move side to side with the ball. If Player 2 volleys to the alley, all four players move to that side.

ball. If you have been pulled wide, your partner must move over and cover the middle. If neither player is moving, the player with the forehand in the middle will usually take the shot. If there is any doubt, go for the ball. Above all, don't be indecisive.

Low Balls

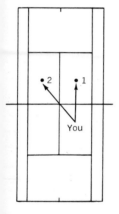

Hit high balls down at feet of nearer player (1).

Hit low balls softly to feet of player farther away (2).

Return the low ball to the feet of the player farther from you. This cross court volley gives the ball more time to drop to your opponent's feet. If you are successful in returning low, move in close, for your opponent must volley up and you will then be in good position to volley down for the winner. Be aggressive and keep attacking. The farther back you stand, the easier it is for your opponents to hit to your feet. Try an angle shot only if you can probably hit it for an outright winner. Don't give your opponents an angle return.

High Balls

If the ball is returned up to you, move in quickly and hit down at the feet of the person nearer to you. The partner who is not hitting is ready to back up the hitting player in case the opponents try a quick lob or lob volley. (The lob volley is a difficult shot, however, and will not often be successful.)

STRATEGY WHEN YOU ARE AT THE NET AND YOUR OPPONENTS ARE BACK

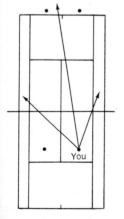

When you are at net and your opponents are back.

Be patient. Realize the rallies will be longer and it will be harder to put the ball away. Don't try to power the ball past your opponents. Short, angled volleys can be effective since they tend to pull one partner up and out of position. If you have no angle, keep the ball deep and down the middle. This will keep your opponents back on defense. Expect the lob. Play farther from the net. Fifteen feet away is not too far back if you don't have much confidence in your overhead. Let the high lobs bounce, but try not to let other lobs get over your head. If the lob should get over one player's head, both partners retreat back. Since your opponents should be moving in, the competitive return is a high defensive lob. If you are hitting the overhead from deep in your court, hit with more spin and less power, and hit it more down the middle. Smash all short lobs and high balls hard and often for the angle.

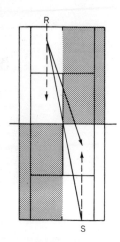

Two-man doubles attack drill. All balls hit diagonally across court (shaded area). Both players move in.

PRACTICING DOUBLES

Beginning Practice

Play slow points (no hard hitting) and emphasize court position. Practice with one player starting at the net on each team. (The net players should poach whenever possible.) Each team should also practice points against a team that has both players back. Each team should practice playing back against a team that has one partner up and the other back, and against a team that has both partners up.

Advanced Practice

Practice against the same situations as in beginning doubles, only play full speed. Add "Aussie" doubles practice for the serving team.

Play full speed attacking points, but with only two players. (This drill develops soft volleys and the feel of attacking. It illustrates the importance of getting to the net quickly.) All balls must be hit to the side of the court diagonally opposite you. Both the server and receiver must come in. Use only second serves, so as to get more balls in play.

BaCKGrounD TO Tennis

HISTORY

Tennis has a rich and intriguing background. Its history has been marred with misfortune, but even kings could not prevent its steady rise in popularity. The development of tennis equipment, facilities, and methods has rightfully made modern tennis one of the world's most interesting and demanding sports.

Tennis is a derivative of a game similar to handball which was played in ancient Greece, Rome, Egypt, Persia, and Arabia. In 13th and 14th century France, tennis was known as "jeu de paume" or "sport of the hands." However, it is believed that its current name is derived from the French word "tenez," meaning "take it" or "play."

A wandering minstrel is thought to have introduced the game to the ladies and noblemen of the French court. The game was played indoors, with a rope cord stretched across the room to serve as a net, or outdoors, across a mound of dirt. At first the open hand was used to bat a cloth bag stuffed with hair back and forth. Later, an all-wood racket, similar to a large ping-pong paddle, was used.

Although Louis IV banned tennis as undignified, it continued to grow in popularity. Louis X again outlawed it, in the 1300's, because he felt "tennis should be thought of as a 'Sport for Kings'."

In the 14th century, tennis moved to England, but there too it had a dubious beginning. It was outlawed because the king felt that his soldiers wasted time playing tennis that they should have spent practicing archery.

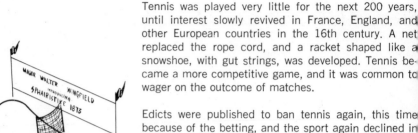

Tennis was played very little for the next 200 years, until interest slowly revived in France, England, and other European countries in the 16th century. A net replaced the rope cord, and a racket shaped like a snowshoe, with gut strings, was developed. Tennis became a more competitive game, and it was common to wager on the outcome of matches.

Edicts were published to ban tennis again, this time because of the betting, and the sport again declined in popularity until by the 19th century only the wealthy were playing the game.

The modern history of tennis began in 1873 when Major Walter Wingfield introduced lawn tennis in England. His was a 15-point game in which only the server could score. Called "sphairistike" after the Greek root for "ball," it was played on an hourglass-shaped court divided by a net seven feet high.

Mary Outerbridge introduced tennis to the United States in 1874. A Bermuda vacation gave her the opportunity to see British soldiers, friends of Wingfield, playing "sphairistike," and, in spite of initial difficulty with United States customs officials, she succeeded in bringing two rackets, a ball, and a net into this country. She was largely responsible for establishing the first court in the United States, on the lawn of the Staten Island Cricket and Baseball Club.

The sport caught on quickly and developed into a vigorous, fast-moving game of skill. In 1881 the United States Lawn Tennis Association was founded to standardize rules pertaining to scoring, size of the ball and racket, and court dimensions. Today, individual players, schools, recreation departments, cities, and clubs belong to the U.S.L.T.A. and the popularity of tennis continues to grow.

COMPETITION

Tennis is in a dynamic state of flux today. Until recently tournaments of any consequence have been open only to amateurs (players ineligible to receive prize money). The limited number of professionals (usually the best one or two amateurs each year "turned pro" in order to play for money) played mostly exhibition matches

Pro!!

throughout the world in a barnstorming fashion. Tournaments, in order to secure the best players, paid so much "under the table" to attract the top amateurs that many amateurs were actually making more money than the pros. In an effort to end this hypocrisy, the British in 1968 made the most important tournament in the world —Wimbledon, held first in 1877—an event "open" to both amateurs and professionals, and offered prize money. The result has been that almost all major international tournaments are now open to both amateurs and professionals. Contract professionals (those playing under contract to a specific promoter), players (a new and probably temporary term for competitors playing for prize money but not under contract to any individual or group), and true amateurs (mostly college age students and under, ineligible for prize money) can compete together in open tournaments. Specific and detailed rules and regulations in the United States may be obtained from the U.S.L.T.A. office (51 E. 42nd St., N. Y. 10017), or from the *U.S.L.T.A. Yearbook and Guide.*

Major World Team Competitions

Contract professionals are currently ineligible for these competitions. The major world team competitions are:

Davis Cup winners:
  Australia
  Britain
  France
  United States

Other countries reaching
the challenge round:
  India
  Italy
  Japan
  Mexico
  Spain
  West Germany

Davis Cup (established in 1900)   Each country annually sends its top male players to compete in dual matches against countries in the same zone. Then the zone winners play, and the eventual winner earns the right to "challenge" the previous year's championship country in the Challenge Round. Each round of play consists of four singles matches and one doubles match.

Wightman Cup (established in 1923)   This trophy is awarded annually to the winner of a dual match between British and American women. Play consists of five singles and two doubles matches.

Federation Cup (established in 1963) The International Lawn Tennis Federation initiated this international team competition for women in which one nation plays another (two singles, one doubles) in a single elimination tournament.

Major World Individual Competitions

The top international tournaments (now all "open" events) are the English Championships (Wimbledon),

Grand Slam

the United States Championships (Forest Hills, New York), the French Championships, and the Australian Championships. Play consists of single elimination type competition. The only players to complete a "grand slam" by winning all four tournaments in the same year are Don Budge and Maureen Connolly of the United States, and Rod Laver and Margaret Smith Court of Australia.

United States Tournament Structure

The United States is divided into 17 sections, all governed by the United States Lawn Tennis Association, but each responsible for promoting and governing tennis competition in its own geographic area. Groupings in local and national competition are by age and sex: youths' under 10, 12, 14, 16, and 18; men's, over 35, 45, 55 and 60; women's, over 35 and 40, all in singles or doubles. Competition also exists in mixed doubles.

Youths may enter a specific age group only if they have not reached the maximum age in that group by January 1st of the year of competition. An adult may play in an age group if he reaches the minimum any time in the year of competition.

Each section has almost weekly competition in most events during the season of play—almost the entire year in some climates. Regular "circuits" of play are established within and between sections and local and

U.S.L.T.A. Sections

Eastern—30 E. 42nd St., New York, NY 10017
Florida—P.O. Box 515, N. Miami, FL 33161
Hawaii—P.O. Box 411, Honolulu, HI 96809
Intermountain—242 Sandrun Road, Salt Lake City, UT 84103
Middle Atlantic—2030 Greenwich St., Falls Church, VA 22043
Middle States—1845 Walnut St., Philadelphia, PA 19103
Missouri Valley—937 45th, Des Moines, IA 50312
New England—22 Wilde Road, Wellesley, MA 02181
Northern California—235 Montgomery, San Francisco, CA 94104
Northwestern—975 Northwestern Bank Bldg., Minneapolis, MN 55402
Pacific Northwest—1040 Logan Bldg., Seattle, WA 98101
Puerto Rico—Banco Credito, San Juan, PR 00905
Southern—3121 Maple Dr., N.E., Atlanta, GA 30305
Southern California—609 N. Cahuenga Blvd., Los Angeles, CA 90004
Southwestern—3003 N. Central, Suite 613, Phoenix, AZ 85012
Texas—3406 W. Lamar St., Houston, TX 77019
Western—69 W. Washington St., Chicago, IL 60602

national rankings in each category are published yearly. Information regarding competition opportunities can be obtained from each section's headquarters.

EQUIPMENT

Racket

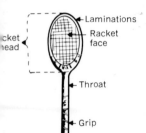

Wood vs. metal   A wood racket consists of many high-grade pieces of wood, put together with glue, heat, and pressure. The racket head is made of plied strips of ash and fiber. The outside strips are often composed of hardwood, such as bamboo. The throat is made of a hardwood, such as maple or birch. The laminations, up to eleven in a good racket, give the racket added strength.

There is quite a difference in how various metal rackets play, especially in their flexibility or stiffness. If you are thinking of purchasing a metal racket, if possible try it out first. Whether to buy a wood or metal racket, though, is mostly a matter of personal preference and has nothing to do with the ability of the player!

Weight   The weight of a racket is something that individual preference should control, but it is usually best to choose the heaviest racket that feels comfortable to you. A general guide is as follows:

> Light weight: 12-13 ounces (girls and women)
> Medium weight: 13½-13¾ ounces (boys and most men)
> Heavy weight: 14-15 ounces (some men)

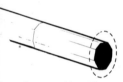

Circumference of handle

Handle size (grip)   The size of the grip is measured by the circumference of the handle. This, along with the general weight classification, is usually marked on the racket by the manufacturer. You should choose the largest grip that feels comfortable. A general guide follows:

> 4¼-4½": young children and girls
> 4½-4⅝": boys and women
> 4⅝-4¾": men

EVENLY BALANCED
APPROVAL SIGN

Balance   Most rackets are evenly balanced. In a 27" racket (the most common length) the balance point is 13½" from the end of the racket. Some people prefer a racket rather light in the head, because it helps their touch when volleying. A player who spends much time at the baseline may prefer a racket slightly heavy in the head, since it tends to afford more power.

Standard string thickness

15-gauge

Tournament thickness

16-gauge

To $10—Beginning with
young child only;
won't last with hard
hitting.
$15-20—Fair frame with
nylon strings;
beginning youth or
adult.
$25-30—Good wood frame
and good nylon
strings or cheap gut,
intermediate youth
or adult.
$30 up—Best wood and gut;
tournament players.
(Metal frames start
around $30 without
strings.)

A press protects the racket
from warping.

Strings   Nylon is relatively durable and cheap ($5-10). Gut provides a better feel, but is more expensive ($10-20) and can be adversely affected by moisture. Generally gut is strung to 55-65 pounds tension, as opposed to nylon's 45-55 pounds.

Fifteen gauge is the standard string thickness but tournament players generally prefer a thinner (16-gauge) string, which wears more rapidly but affords more feel. Individual strings may usually be replaced at a nominal cost.

Cost   Rackets cost anywhere between $5.00 and $60.00 (with strings). A beginning adult should purchase a medium grade racket, pre-strung with a medium grade nylon, for $12.00-$20.00. An intermediate or advanced adult who is serious about tennis should probably not spend less than $15.00 for a racket frame (without strings).

Care   Metal rackets cost more but tend to last longer and require virtually no care. The use of laminations has greatly reduced the need for special care of a wood racket, but it should be kept in a press if it is subjected to much moisture or if it is to be stored for a long period of time.

A single layer of adhesive tape around the edge of the racket head can help to keep exposed strings from wear due to contact of the racket with the ground.

Balls

Tennis balls are made from rubber molded into two cups which are cemented together and covered with wool felt. Some balls are covered with extra felt for increased wear and are called "heavy duty" balls. The best balls are inflated with compressed air or gas which gives them their resiliency. Some balls now receive at least some of their resiliency from the rubber that is used.

Specifications   The official ball is approximately 2½" in diameter and weighs 2 ounces. It should bounce approximately 55" when dropped from 100".

Care   The ball can should not be opened until ready for use, since it is pressure sealed to help retain the pressure within the ball. Even when kept in an unopened

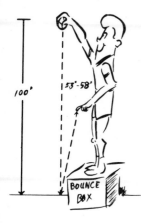

can for an excessive period, the compression is gradually reduced, and the ball tends to "deaden."

The felt of a good ball will wear, making the ball considerably lighter after two or three hard sets. For this reason, balls are changed every nine games or so in a championship tournament. For non-competitive play, however, the life of an otherwise good ball may be temporarily restored by putting the ball through a cycle in a clothes washer and dryer.

Dress

The traditional tennis costume is all white, mainly because white reflects heat better than other colors and is thus cooler. Men wear shorts, shirt (always), tennis shoes, sweater or jacket, socks, cap, and wrist band (perspiration absorbent and worn by top players to help keep perspiration from eyes and hands). Women wear the same, except that most women favor a blouse and shorts or a tennis dress.

TYPES OF COURTS

The type of court is largely determined by the climate and traditions of a particular location. The court may be indoors or outdoors, and may be grass, soft court ("clay"), or hardcourt. A canvas, "plastic" saran, hedge, or wooden slat "fencing" often surrounds the court to aid in reducing the wind and increase visibility of the ball.

Court and fencing

Court diagram

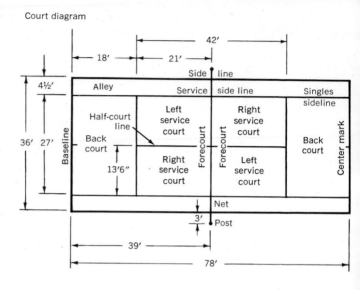

Grass Courts

Grass provides a popular traditional court surface, a carryover from the early days of the game when people would erect a net and play in their yards.

Today it is the world's least common surface, though the Wimbledon, Australian, and United States Championships and many of the major world tournaments are still played on grass. Most of the grass courts in the United States are located in the East.

Advantages   Most players enjoy playing on a grass court. The style of play is more aggressive than on clay, as the ball tends to skid and bounce low. The grass surface encourages net play, largely because of the ever-present possibility of bad bounces.

Disadvantages   Grass courts require constant maintenance. The grass must be clipped smooth and kept watered, and the lines need frequent remarking. When the courts are damp, the ball becomes heavy and wet. The courts are rather slippery, and some players wear spikes on their tennis shoes to aid footing. Where the turf is worn, bounces become irregular and unpredictable.

Soft Courts

In areas where grass doesn't grow well, or where it is difficult to secure composition materials, dirt or clay is a common court surface. Most of the world's tennis courts are classified as "soft" courts and are a clay-like material. In the United States the South has a high proportion of clay courts.

Advantages   Clay courts are easy on the feet. The style of play is slightly slower, and less emphasis is placed on attack. The ball bounces higher and more slowly off the court, so the player has more time to run and prepare for his shot.

Disadvantages   The clay court is difficult to keep in top playing condition. It must be watered and rolled daily, the chalk lines need remarking regularly, or tape lines need to be swept or reset.

Hardcourts

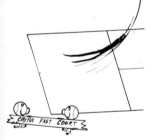

Courts of asphalt, cement, wood, and composition materials are classified as hardcourts. Internationally, it is the least common surface, and the United States is the only major tennis country with a majority of hardcourts. This is almost the only type of court in the Western United States.

Advantages   The ball bounces uniformly. A minimum of upkeep is required, although an asphalt court should be resurfaced every four or five years. The courts often are painted to facilitate visibility, usually a green court bordered by a red area surrounding the playing lines.

Disadvantages   The primary disadvantage is that it is not the standard court throughout the world. Some people object to the extremely aggressive type of play possible on the faster court, that the ball rebounds too quickly from the playing surface.

Percent of hardcourts in several leading tennis countries.

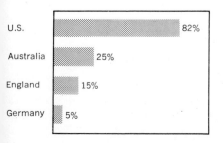

U.S.	82%
Australia	25%
England	15%
Germany	5%

Of the balance, about half are soft courts and half grass courts.

ETIQUETTE

Spectator Conduct

Whether you are a casual spectator watching an informal match or a member of a large crowd watching a championship tournament, you should be aware of some "unwritten rules." Player concentration is essential to a top performance, and anything which detracts from this concentration could affect the outcome of an entire match. The general rule is to govern your actions the way you would want others to act if you were playing.

Some specific rules to follow are:
1. Remain seated in the areas provided for spectators. Never sit on any benches or seats within the fenced area unless you have a specific function.
2. Keep quiet. Nothing is more disturbing than unnecessary conversation.
3. Applaud good play after the point is completed.
4. If you are interested in the score, keep it yourself. Do not continually bother the players by asking the score.
5. If you disagree with a decision, keep your opinion to yourself.
6. Referee a match only if acting in that official capacity. (If you are asked to serve as an umpire or linesman, you should do so willingly.)
7. If you are heading for another court, walk inconspicuously behind the fence of the court where play is in progress.

Player Conduct

Good sportsmanship is the key to tennis etiquette. Treat others as you desire to be treated.

Greet your opponent

The following are some specific rules that will make tennis more enjoyable for you and for those around you:
1. Know your opponent. Before you play, greet your opponent and introduce yourself.
2. Spin your racket to decide the choice of serve and side before you walk onto the court.
3. Check the net height at the center of the court. The net is 36 inches high. If you have a standard sized

Check the net height

Control temper

Retrieve all balls

racket, stand your racket on the ground by the handle (27″) and place the edge of the racket head of your opponent (9″) on the top of your racket head.

4. After a brief warm-up (5-minute maximum), ask your opponent if he wishes to practice any serves. All practice serves should be taken by both players before any points are played. Never take the "first one in."

5. Begin a point as a server only if you have two balls in your hand.

6. Wait until your opponent is ready before serving.

7. Failure to observe the footfault rule is considered a breach of tennis etiquette.

8. Keep score accurately and, as server, periodically announce the score.

9. Return only balls that are good, especially on the serve.

10. Call the balls on your side of the net (say "out" if the ball is out), and trust your opponent to do the same. Call faults and lets loud and clear. If the ball is in, or if you are unsure, you must play the ball as good and say nothing.

11. Talk only when pertinent to the match; and then only when the ball is not in play. However, recognize a good play by your partner or opponent.

12. Control your feelings and temper.

13. Collect all balls on your side of the net after each point and return them directly to the server. Don't lean on the net to retrieve a ball—the net cables break easily. When the match is completed, leave no balls or debris on the court.

14. Retrieve balls from an adjacent court by waiting until the point is over and then politely by saying "Thank you" or "Ball, please."

15. Return balls from an adjacent court by waiting until the play in progress has been completed, and then by tossing or rolling them to the nearest player.

16. Call a "let" when there is reasonable interference during play (such as another ball entering your court).

17. Make no excuses. At the conclusion of play, shake hands with your opponent, and thank him for the match. Congratulate him if he won.

18. If others are waiting, don't monopolize the courts. Either play doubles or rotate at the conclusion of each set.

19. Always dress properly—neat and in all white and wearing a shirt.

Tournament Conduct

1. Report to the tournament desk at least 15 minutes ahead of scheduled time. If you cannot, let the tournament desk know ahead that you must default
2. The winner returns all balls to the tournament desk, reports the score, and ascertains his next playing time.
3. Offer to help the tournament committee (call lines, prepare courts, transportation, etc.).
4. Thank the tournament director at the end of the tourney. If room and board were provided, thank adequately those responsible.

RULES OF TENNIS

The governing body of international tennis is the International Lawn Tennis Federation (Barons Court, West Kensington, London, W.14, England). This federation establishes the rules of tennis, and the United States Lawn Tennis Association, as a member of this organization, subscribes to these rules. Portions of them follow:

Server and Receiver

The players stand on opposite sides of the net. The player who first delivers the ball is called the server, and the other the receiver.

Choice of Service or Side

Spin the racket to decide who choses first.

"M" or "W"

The choice of sides and the right to be server or receiver in the first game is decided by toss. Generally one player spins his racket and the other player calls one of the options presented by the markings on the racket ("upside-down" or "right-side-up," "M" or "W," "number" or "no number," and so on). The player winning the toss may choose, or require the opponent to choose:

a) The right to be server or receiver, in which case the other player chooses the side; or
b) The side, in which case the other player chooses the right to be server or receiver.

Players change sides after the games played in each set total an odd number—after the first game and every two games thereafter. A maximum of one minute is allowed for players to change sides.

Faults

The serve is a fault:
a) If the server fails to hit the ball into the proper court.
b) If the server misses the ball in attempting to strike it. (It may be tossed several times without penalty.)
c) If the ball served touches a permanent fixture (other than the net) or the server's partner before it hits the ground.
d) If a footfault is committed.

A footfault is called:
a) If the server changes his position by walking or running before he hits the ball. (A server may jump at the serve, and one or both feet may be over the baseline, provided he does not touch the court or line before contacting the ball.)
b) If the server touches the baseline or the court area within the baseline before he hits the ball.
c) If the server serves from outside the area between the sideline and the center mark.

Foot faults

Lets

A let is a served ball which touches the net, strap, or band, and is otherwise good. A let is called when play is interrupted or if the serve is delivered before the receiver is ready. (If the receiver attempts to return the ball, he is deemed ready.)

When a let occurs on a service, the serve is replayed. When a let occurs during a play other than on a serve, the play continues uninterrupted.

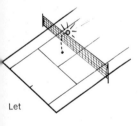

Let

When Receiver Becomes Server

At the conclusion of a game, the server becomes the receiver and the receiver becomes the server.

When Player Loses Point

A player loses the point if:
a) He serves a double fault.
b) He fails to return the ball before it bounces twice (it may be hit before it bounces or after it bounces once only), or if he does not return it into his opponent's court.
c) He returns the ball so that it hits the ground, a permanent fixture (fence, umpire's stand), or other object outside any of the lines which bound his opponent's court.

d) He volleys the ball and fails to make a good return even when standing outside the court.
e) He touches the ball in play with his racket more than once when making a stroke. (In doubles, the ball may be returned by only one partner.)
f) He or his racket or anything he wears or carries touches the net or the ground within the opponent's court.
g) He volleys the ball before it has passed the net.
h) The ball in play touches him or anything he wears or carries except his racket.
i) He throws his racket at and hits the ball.
j) He deliberately commits any act which hinders his opponent in making a stroke.

Ball lands on line

Good Return

It is a good return if:
a) The ball lands on the line.
b) The ball touches the net, provided it passes over it and lands in the proper court.
c) The player reaches over the net to hit a ball that has blown or rebounded back to the other side of its own accord, provided the player does not touch the net with his racket, body, or clothing.
d) The player's racket passes over the net after the ball has been returned, provided the net is not touched.
e) The player returns a ball which has hit a ball lying in the court. (A player may request a ball lying in his opponent's court to be removed, but not while the ball is in play.)
f) The ball is returned outside the post, either above or below the level of the net, provided it lands in the proper court, even though it touches the post.

Ball hits top of net post and bounces into the court.

Order of Service in Doubles

The order of serving is decided at the beginning of each set. The pair who serve in the first game of each set decide which partner shall do so. The other partner serves the third game. The opposing pair decide who shall serve the second game of the set. The partner then serves the fourth game. This order is followed throughout the set so that each player will serve every fourth game.

If a player serves out of turn, the correct player must serve as soon as the mistake is discovered. All points

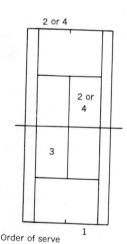

Order of serve

earned are counted. If a complete game is played with
the wrong player serving, the order of serve remains as
altered.

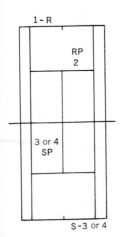

Order of receiving

Order of Receiving in Doubles

The order for receiving is determined at the beginning
of each set. The receiving pair decide who is to receive
the first point, and that player continues to receive the
serves directed to that particular service court throughout the set. (In other words, he receives every other
point in every other game.) The other partner does the
same to the serves directed to the other service court.

If a player receives out of turn, he remains in that position until the game in which it is discovered is completed. The partners then resume their original positions.

SCORING

The Scoring of a Game

Points are called as follows, with the server's score always called first:

> 0 points — love
> 1st point — 15
> 2nd point — 30
> 3rd point — 40
> 4th point — game

The chart in the margin illustrates possible scoring
combinations. "Deuce" means that each side has won
three points. One side must now win two consecutive
points to win the game. The first point after deuce is
called "advantage." If the server wins it, the score is
called "advantage (ad) in." If the receiver wins the first
point after deuce, the score is called "advantage" (ad)
out."

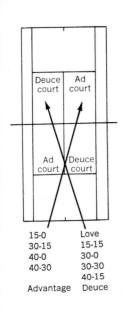

15-0	Love
30-15	15-15
40-0	30-0
40-30	30-30
	40-15
Advantage	Deuce

The Scoring of a Set

Conventionally, the side first winning six games wins
the set, provided it is ahead by at least two games. (If
the score is 5-5 [5-all], play continues until someone
gets two games ahead—7-5, 8-6, etc.) An average set
takes about 30 minutes to complete.

Tie break scoring   To help eliminate extended sets
(20-18, etc.) the U.S.L.T.A. has recently authorized a

Even the umpire can't keep up with new "sudden death" scoring methods.

SET	TED	SAM
1	6	3
2	5	7
3	11	9

best of nine point tie break system that can be used when the score reaches 6-6 in any set. (A best of twelve point system may also be used.) The new "sudden death" system is played as follows:

In singles, player A, due to serve the next regular game, serves two points, the first to the deuce court and the second to the ad court. Then player B does the same. Sides are changed after four points and the service sequence is repeated. If neither side has won five points, player B serves point nine. The receiver may elect to receive from either the right or left court. The set ends at 7-6. The players stay on the same side, and player B serves, the first game of the next set.

In doubles (Team A-B vs. C-D), A and C serve the first 4 points and B and D the next 4. Player D serves the ninth point if needed. Players serve from the same sides they have been serving from.

VASSS   The VASSS system is not an official scoring system for championship matches, but it is used extensively otherwise. It is basically a "ping pong" scoring system to a 31 point set, with the serve changing every 5 points. Its advantage is that it also prevents long, drawn-out matches.

The Scoring of a Match

A match is completed when one person or side wins two of three sets, although in top men's tournaments a match usually consists of three of five sets. A ten minute break is allowed between the third and fourth sets, and is mandatory between the second and third sets for all youth events 16 years of age and under.

Server has won:	Receiver has won:	Score is:
1 point	0 point	15-love
2	0	30-love
3	0	40-love
4	0	game
3	1	40-15
3	2	40-30
1	1	15-all
2	2	30-all
3	3	deuce
4	3	ad in
3	4	ad out
5	3	game (server)

GLOSSary OF Tennis Terms

American Twist

Ace. A ball that is served so well that the opponent fails to touch it with his racket.

Ad. Short for advantage. It is the first point scored after deuce. If the serving side scores, it is "ad in"; if the receiving side, it is "ad out."

Ad court. The left service court, so called because an "ad" score is served there.

All. An even score: 30-all, 3-all, etc.

Alley. The area on either side of the singles court which enlarges the width of the court for doubles. Each alley is 4½ feet wide.

American Twist. A serve in which the ball bounces high and in the opposite direction from which it was originally traveling.

Angle shot. A ball hit to an extreme angle across the court.

Approach. A shot behind which a player comes to the net.

Attack drive. An aggressive approach shot.

Australian doubles. Doubles in which the point begins with the server and his partner on the same side of the court.

Back court. The area between the service line and the baseline.

Backhand. The stroke used to return balls hit to the left of a righthanded player.

Backhand court. The left side of the court (for a right-handed player).

Backspin. Spin from bottom to top, applied by hitting down and through the ball. Also called underspin. *See also* Slice, Chop.

Backswing. The initial part of any swing. The act of bringing the racket back to prepare for the forward swing.

Ball boy. A person who retrieves balls for tennis players during competition.

Baseline. The end boundary line of a tennis court, located 39 feet from the net.

Break service. To win a game in which the opponent serves.

Bye. The state, in competition, in which a player is not required to play in a particular round.

Cannonball. A hard, flat serve.

Center mark. The short line that bisects the center of the baseline.

Center service line. The line which is perpendicular to the net and divides the two service courts.

Center strap. A strap in the center of the net, anchored to the ground to hold the net secure.

Chip. A modified slice, used primarily in doubles to return a serve. A chip requires a short swing, which allows the receiver to move in close to return.

Choke. To grip the racket up toward the head.

Chop. A backspin shot in which the racket moves down through the ball at greater than a 45 degree angle.

Closed face. The angle of the hitting face of the racket when it is turned down toward the court.

Consolation. A tournament in which first round losers continue to play in a losers' tournament.

Cross court shot. A shot in which the ball travels diagonally across the net, from one corner to the other.

Deep shot. A shot that bounces near the baseline (near the service line on a serve).

Default. Failure to complete a scheduled match in a tournament; such a player forfeits his position.

Deuce. A score of 40-40 (the score is tied and each side has at least three points).

Deuce court. Right court, so called because a deuce score is served there.

Dink. A ball hit so that it floats back with extreme softness.

Double elimination. A tournament in which you must lose twice before you are eliminated.

Double fault. The failure of both service attempts to be good. It costs a point.

Doubles. A match with four players, two on each team.

Draw. The means of establishing who plays whom in a tournament.

Drive. An offensive ball hit with force.

Drop shot. A softly hit shot that barely travels over the net.

Drop volley. A drop shot that is hit from a volley position.

Choke

Earned point. A point won by skillful playing rather than by a player's mistake.

Elimination. A tournament in which one is eliminated when defeated.

Error. A point which ends by an obvious mistake rather than by skillful playing.

Face. The hitting surface of the racket.

Fast court. A smooth surfaced court, which allows the ball to bounce quickly and low.

Fault. An improper hit, generally thought of as a serve error.

Fifteen. The first point won by a player.

Flat shot. A shot that travels in a straight line with little arc and little spin.

Floater. A ball that moves slowly across the net in a high trajectory.

Foot fault. A fault caused by the server stepping on or over the baseline before hitting the ball in service.

Force. A ball hit with exceptional power. A play in which, because of the speed and placement of the shot, the opponent is pulled out of position.

Forecourt. The area between the net and the service line.

Forehand. The stroke used to return balls hit to the right of a righthanded player.

Forehand court. The right side of the court for a right-handed player.

Forty. A player's score when he has won three points.

Frame. The part of the racket which holds the strings.

Game. That part of a set that is completed when one player or side wins four points, or wins two consecutive points after deuce.

Grip. The method of holding the racket handle. The term given the leather covering on the handle.

Ground strokes. Strokes made after the ball has bounced, either forehand or backhand.

Ground Strokes

    Drive
    Slice and Chop
    Lob
    Drop shot

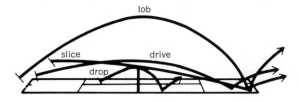

Gut. Racket strings made from animal intestines.

Half volley. Hitting the ball immediately after it bounces from the court.

Handle. The part of the racket that is gripped in the hand.

Racket head

Head. The part of the racket used to hit the ball; includes the frame and the strings.

Hold serve. To serve and to win that game.

Kill. To smash the ball down hard.

Let. A point played over because of interference. A serve which hits the top of the net but is otherwise good.

Linesman. A person responsible for calling balls that land outside the court in competition.

Lob. A ball hit high enough in the air (usually clearing the net by at least eight feet) to pass over the head of the net player.

Love. Zero; no score.

Love game. A game won without the loss of a point.

Love set. A set won without the loss of a game.

Match. Singles or doubles play that consists of two out of three sets for all women's and most men's matches, or three out of five sets for most men's championship matches.

Match point. The point which, if won, wins the match for a player.

Midcourt. The general area in the center of the playing court, midway between the net and baseline.

Mix up. To vary the type of shots attempted.

Net game. The play at the net. Also called net play.

Net Play

    Drive volley
    Half volley
      (and Low volley)
    Drop volley
    Overhead smash

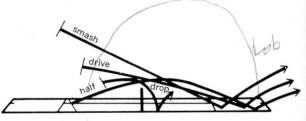

Net man. The partner in doubles who plays at the net.

No Man's Land. Midcourt, where many balls bounce at the player's feet and he is unusually vulnerable.

Open face. The angle of the hitting face of the racket when it is turned up, away from the court surface.

Opening. A defensive mistake which allows an opponent a good chance to score a point.

Out. A ball landing outside the playing court.

Overhead smash. *See* Smash

Overspin. *See* Topspin

Pace. Speed; usually the speed or spin of a ball which makes it skip quickly.

Passing shot.   A ball hit out of reach of a net player.

Percentage tennis.   "Conservative" tennis that emphasizes cutting down on unnecessary errors and on errors at critical points.

Place.   To hit the ball to the desired area.

Placement.   A shot placed so accurately that an opponent cannot reach it.

Poach.   A strategy whereby the net player in doubles moves over to his serving partner's side of the court to make a volley.

Press.   The wooden frame that holds a wood tennis racket firmly to prevent warping.

Rally.   Play in exclusion of the serve.

Retrieve.   A good return of a difficult shot.

Round robin.   A tournament in which every player plays every other player.

Rush.   To advance to the net after hitting an approach shot.

Seed.   To arrange tournament matches so that top players don't play together until the final rounds.

Serve (Service).   Method of starting point.

Serve

   Flat
   Topspin
   Slice
   American twist

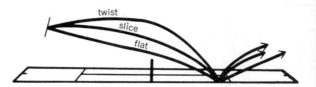

Service line.   The line which outlines the base of the service court; parallel to the baseline and 21 feet from the net.

Set.   That part of a match that is completed when one player or side wins at least six games and is ahead by at least two games, or has won the tie break.

Set point.   The point which, if won, will win the set.

Sidespin.   A shot in which the ball spins to the side and bounces to the side. The sidespin slice is one of the most common types of serve.

Singles.   A match between two players.

Slice.   A backspin shot that is hit with the racket traveling down through the ball at less than a 45 degree angle with the ground. *See also* Chip.

Slow court.   A court with a rough surface which tends to make the ball bounce rather high and slow.

Smash.   A hard overhead shot.

Spin.   Rotation of the ball caused by hitting it at an angle. *See* Topspin, Sidespin, Backspin

Straight sets.   To win a match without the loss of a set.

Tape.   The canvas band which runs across the top of the net.

Tennis elbow.   A painful condition in the elbow joint, common to tennis players and caused mostly by hyper-extension of the arm.

Thirty.   The term which means that a player has scored two points.

Throat.   The part of the racket between the handle and the head.

Tie break.   An official nine point or best of twelve point sudden death scoring system when the score is 6 games-all.

Topspin.   Spin of the ball from top to bottom; caused by hitting up and through the ball. It makes the ball bounce fast and long and is used on most ground strokes.

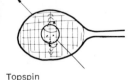

Topspin

Trajectory.   The flight of the ball in relation to the top of the net.

Umpire.   The person who officiates at major matches.

Undercut.   A backspin caused by hitting down through the ball.

Underspin.   *See* Backspin, Slice, Chop.

Unseeded.   The players not favored to win and not given any special place on the draw in a tournament.

VASSS.   An unofficial ping-pong (31-point) scoring system to prevent long extended sets.

Volley.   To hit the ball before it bounces.

Wood shot.   A ball hit on the wood of the racket.

Umpire

BIBLIOGraPHY

BOOKS

Addie, Pauline Betz. *Tennis for Teenagers.* Washington, D.C.: Acropolis, 1966.

Barnaby, John M. *Racket Work: The Key to Tennis.* Rockleigh, N.J.: Allyn, 1969.

Budge, Don. *Don Budge: A Tennis Memoir.* New York: Viking, 1969.

Budge, Lloyd. *Tennis Made Easy.* New York: Ronald, 1945.

Cummings, Parke. *American Tennis.* Boston: Little, Brown, 1957.

Cutler, Merritt M. *The Tennis Book.* New York: McGraw-Hill, 1967.

Davies, Mike. *Lawn Tennis.* New York: Arc Books, 1963.

Driver, Helen I. *Tennis for Teachers.* Madison, Wisc.: Monona-Driver, 1970.

————. *Tennis Self Instructor.* Madison, Wisc.: Monona-Driver, 1966.

Everett, Peter and Skillman, Virginia D. *Beginning Tennis.* Belmont, Calif.: Wadsworth, 1968.

Faulkner, Edwin J. and Weymuller, Frederick. *Tennis: How to Play It, How to Teach It.* New York: Dial, 1970.

Fiske, Loring. *How to Beat Better Tennis Players.* Garden City, N.Y.: Doubleday, 1970.

Gibson, Althea. *I Always Wanted to be Somebody.* New York: Harper, 1958.

Gonzales, Pancho. *Tennis.* New York: Fleet, 1962.

Harman, Bob and Monroe, Keith. *Use Your Head in Tennis.* Port Washington, N.Y.: Kennikat, 1950.

Jacobs, Helen Hull. *Gallery of Champions.* New York: Barnes, 1949.

Johnson, Joan and Xanthos, Paul. *Tennis.* Dubuque, Iowa: Brown, 1967.

Jones, C. M. *How to Become a Champion.* Levittown, N.Y.: Transatlantic, 1968.

Kenfield, John F., Jr. *Teaching and Coaching Tennis.* Dubuque, Iowa: Brown, 1964.

King, Billie Jean. *Tennis to Win.* New York: Harper, 1970.

Laney, Al. *Covering the Court.* New York: Simon & Schuster, 1968.

Lardner, Rex. *The Underhanded Serve.* New York: Hawthorn, 1968.

Laver, Rod and Pollard, Jack. *How to Play Championship Tennis.* New York: Macmillan, 1970.

McPhee, John. *Levels of the Game.* New York: Farrar, 1959.

Metzler, Paul. *Advanced Tennis.* New York: Sterling, 1968.

_____. *Tennis Styles and Stylists.* New York: Macmillan, 1970.

Mulloy, Gardnar. *The Will to Win.* New York: Barnes, 1960.

Murphy, Bill and Murphy, Chet. *Tennis for Beginners.* New York: Ronald, 1958.

_____. *Tennis Handbook.* New York: Ronald 1962.

Murphy, Chet. *Advanced Tennis.* Dubuque, Iowa: Brown, 1970.

Palfrey, Sarah. *Tennis for Anyone.* New York: Simon & Schuster, 1970.

Pelton, Barry C. *Tennis.* Pacific Palisades, Calif.: Goodyear, 1969.

Plagenhoef, Stan. *Fundamentals of Tennis.* Englewood Cliffs, N.J.: Prentice-Hall, 1970.

Potter, Edward C. *Kings of the Court.* New York: Barnes, 1963.

Ramo, Simon. *Extraordinary Tennis for the Ordinary Player.* New York: Crown, 1970.

Richards, Gilbert. *Tennis for Travelers.* Cincinnati: Tennis, 1969.

Riessen, Clare. *Tennis: A Basic Guide.* New York: Lothrop, 1969.

Sports Illustrated Book of Tennis. Philadelphia: Lippincott, 1960.

Talbert, Bill and Axtheim, Pete. *Tennis Observed.* Barre, Mass.: Barre, 1967.

Talbert, Bill and Greer, Gordon. *Bill Talbert's Weekend Tennis.* Garden City, N.Y.: Doubleday, 1970.

Talbert, William F. and Old, Bruce S. *The Game of Doubles in Tennis.* Philadelphia: Lippincott, 1968.

_____. *The Game of Singles in Tennis.* Philadelphia: Lippincott, 1962.

Tilden, William T. *Match Play and the Spin of the Ball.* Port Washington, N.Y.: Kennikat, 1968.

Trengove, Alan, ed. *How to Play Tennis the Professional Way.* New York: Simon & Schuster, 1964.

United States Lawn Tennis Association. *The Official USLTA Yearbook and Tennis Guide.* New York: H. O. Zimman, annual.

Wilder, Roy. *Friend of Tennis.* New York: H. O. Zimman, 1962.

MAGAZINES

American Lawn Tennis, East Carolina Avenue, Clinton, SC 29325

Lawn Tennis Magazine, Lowlands, Wenhasten, Halesworth, Suffolk, England

Tennis Magazine, Box 805, Highland Park, IL 60035

Tennis U.S.A., USLTA, 51 East 42nd Street, New York, NY 10017

Tennis West, P.O. Box 5048, Santa Monica, CA 90405

Tennis World, 116a High Street, Bechenham, Kent, England

World Tennis, 8100 Westglen, Houston, TX 77042

FILMS (16mm)

Anyone for Tennis (color). USLTA, 51 East 42nd Street, New York, NY 10017

Beginning Tennis. All-American Productions, P.O. Box 91, Greeley, CO 80632

Beginning Tennis (color). The Athletic Institute, 805 Merchandise Mart, Chicago, IL 60654

Championship Tennis (color, 20 min.). Tennis Associates, 13170 Lorene Court, Mt. View, CA 94040

Elementary Fundamentals (b&w, color). All-American Productions, P.O. Box 91, Greeley, CO 80632

Elementary Tennis (color, 15 min.). Dennis Van der Meer, World Tennis, Box 3, Gracie Station, New York, NY 10028

Fundamentals of Tennis (b&w). University of Arizona, Tucson, AZ 85721

Great Moments in the History of Tennis. American Safety Razor Co., Phillip Morris, Inc., 100 Park Avenue, New York, NY 10017

The How To's of Tennis. Wheaties Sports Federation, Title Insurance Bldg., Minneapolis, MN 55401

Intermediate and Advanced Fundamentals (b&w, color). All-American Productions, P.O. Box 91, Greeley, CO 80632

Intermediate and Advanced Tennis (b&w). T. N. Rogers Productions, 6641 Clearsprings Rd., Santa Susana, CA 93063

Tennis Class Organization (color, 25 min.). USLTA, 51 East 42nd Street, New York, NY 10017

Tennis for Beginners (b&w, color). USLTA, 51 East 42nd Street, New York, NY 10017

Tennis for Everybody (b&w, color). Allegro Film Productions, 201 West 52nd Street, New York, NY 10019

Tennis Fundamentals (color). Tennis Films International, Inc., 137 Newbury Street, Boston, MA 02116

Tennis — A Game of a Lifetime (b&w, 19 min.). USLTA, 51 East 42nd Street, New York, NY 10017

Tennis — Sport of a Lifetime. Part One: Class Organization (color, 30 min.). Youth Tennis Foundation of Southern California, 609 West Cahuenga Blvd., Los Angeles, CA 90028

Tennis Techniques (color, 12 min.). T. N. Rogers Productions, 6641 Clearsprings Road, Santa Susana, CA 93063

The Way to Wimbledon (b&w, color, 20 min.). British Information Services, 45 Rockefeller Plaza, New York, NY 10020

Write the USLTA for information on Davis Cup and USLTA singles championship films. Tennis films for loan or purchase are also available from the Nestle Sports Foundation (Attn: Carol Webb), Slazenger Film Dept., 5-7 John Princes St., London, W.1, England.